International Environmental Law and Distributive Justice

The Clean Development Mechanism (CDM) is widely regarded as one of the Kyoto Protocol's best creations and as an essential part of the international climate change regime. The CDM has been constantly evolving to ensure that it fulfils its objectives of mitigating climate change and contributing to sustainable development in developing countries. The more than 6,000 registered projects under the CDM are estimated to have generated almost US$200 billion of investment in developing countries and are expected to achieve greenhouse gas (GHG) emission reductions of about 6.8 billion tonnes. Nevertheless, the CDM is not perfect, and one of its main problems is the inequitable geographic distribution of projects among developing countries. Understandably, this is a problem that countries are very keen to address, and, since 2001, even before the first project was registered, countries have been highlighting the need to ensure that projects are equitably distributed among participating countries.

This book looks at distributive justice under the CDM regime and focuses on the issue of equity in the geographic distribution of CDM projects among developing countries. The book investigates relevant aspects of international law to identify the legal characteristics of equitable distribution or distributive justice, in order to establish what equitable distribution in the CDM should look like. Based on these investigations, Tomilola Akanle Eni-Ibukun breaks new ground in defining equitable distribution under the CDM and exploring how key obstructions to the equitable distribution of projects may be overcome.

The book will be of particular interest to academics and policymakers concerned with climate change and the CDM within international law.

Tomilola Akanle Eni-Ibukun is an environmental lawyer and researcher, with a PhD in law from the University of Dundee. Her expertise is in sustainable development and climate change law, including the CDM. She is also a barrister and solicitor of the Supreme Court of Nigeria, and is currently the Manager and Editor of the International Institute for Sustainable Development's Conference Reporting Services.

Routledge Research in International Environmental Law

Available titles in this series:

Forthcoming titles in this series:

International Environmental Law and Distributive Justice

Tomilola Akanle Eni-Ibukun

R Routledge
Taylor & Francis Group

LONDON AND NEW YORK

First published 2014
by Routledge
2 Park Square, Milton Park, Abingdon, Oxfordshire OX14 4RN

and by Routledge
711 Third Avenue, New York, NY 10017

First issued in paperback 2015

Routledge is an imprint of the Taylor & Francis Group, an informa business

British Library Cataloguing in Publication Data
A catalogue record for this book is available from the British Library

Library of Congress Cataloging-in-Publication Data
A catalog record has been requested for this book

ISBN13: 978-1-138-93749-9 (pbk)
ISBN13: 978-0-415-65960-4 (hbk)

Typeset in Sabon by
Florence Production Ltd, Stoodleigh, Devon, UK

Contents

Foreword

As a former climate change negotiator, Chair of the Executive Board of the Clean Development Mechanism (CDM) and now Director of a UN programme supporting market mechanisms and approaches to combat climate change, I can attest that enhancing the regional distribution of CDM projects has been a high priority of the designers and implementers of the mechanism since its establishment. The challenge is worth addressing, because the CDM itself holds many benefits, and it is only right that those benefits be enjoyed around the developing world.

However, CDM projects have for the most part gone to where the emissions are and to where the capacity exists to set up projects. Let me be clear, this is a great success of the CDM. It has done exactly what it was designed to do: produce emission reductions that can help countries achieve compliance with their obligations under the Kyoto Protocol. In this respect, the mechanism has been outstanding, creating to date almost 7,000 projects in eighty-six developing countries, everything from renewable energy projects, to efficient cookstove projects, to projects that reduce emissions of potent industrial gases. In so doing, CDM projects have produced more than 1.3 billion saleable certified emission reduction credits. It is in its other objective, that of assisting developing countries to achieve their sustainable development goals, and more specifically of spreading this benefit to less-developed countries, that the mechanism has been challenged. Hence, the great value in considering the issues and recommendations in this book, to inform not only the ongoing evolution of the CDM, but also the development of future market mechanisms and approaches. I am thinking now of the book's service in defining equitable distribution of projects and its care in stressing the need to preserve the CDM's private-sector appeal when instituting any changes to target those countries that have not yet benefited from the mechanism.

A great deal has been done to improve the regional distribution of the CDM, such as targeted capacity building, a loan scheme to help in the preparation of project design documents, creation of emissions baseline and monitoring methodologies targeted at underrepresented regions, and the streamlining of processes through which to vet projects, especially smaller projects. Actually, the past few years have seen fundamental changes in the CDM that can be expected to scale up and extend the reach of the mechanism. These include programmes of activities that allow an unlimited number of project activities to be administered under a single programme umbrella, thus allowing for smaller projects and reduced administrative burden, and approval of rules for standardised baselines, which will add clarity and thus efficiency in vetting potential projects. The CDM board has also just joined with cooperating agencies to set up regional collaboration centres that will allow on-the-ground support to potential project participants.

This book considers how to further improve the distribution of CDM projects among countries, making several recommendations to this end. This work is most welcome and comes at a crucial time in the evolution of the CDM, when the modalities and procedures of the mechanism are under review by parties to the Kyoto Protocol. For this timely and useful contribution, I thank the author and wish that her work will receive the wide readership that it deserves.

Dr John Kilani
Director, Sustainable Development Mechanisms
United Nations Framework Convention on Climate Change

Preface

Within a period of just 10 years, the Clean Development Mechanism (CDM) has exceeded most expectations for its performance, reducing millions of tonnes of carbon dioxide and raising billions of dollars in investment for developing countries. However, it faces several criticisms, one of which is that CDM projects and the benefits they bring are inequitably distributed among developing countries.

This problem has long stumped countries and researchers, who have proposed and implemented various measures to address it, but with limited success. A large part of the problem they have faced in attempting to address the inequitable distribution is that the exact nature of the problem has yet to be defined. First is the question of what an equitable distribution should look like. Without this primary idea, it is impossible to know whether or not the current distribution actually is inequitable. Then there is the question of whether an equitable distribution of projects is possible. The fact that the various measures to address this problem have had limited success may indicate that it is not. If an equitable distribution is possible, then the question becomes, how can it be achieved? What are the key challenges to achieving an equitable distribution of projects under the CDM?

This book addresses all of these questions. The goal of the book is to set out how to ensure that more countries, particularly those that are in greatest need, can increase their participation in the CDM and enjoy its benefits. In the book, I dispel any suggestion that the CDM should not seek to achieve equity in its distribution, but, rather, should focus just on achieving climate mitigation wherever it is cheapest. I show that it *is* possible to achieve equity, if only there is concerted effort to ensure that the CDM achieves its objectives. In addition, as policymakers are working on a new market mechanism, to ensure the buy-in of all countries, it would be important to reassure them that they will benefit from this new market mechanism. I believe this book shows how this can be achieved.

This book is based on my PhD thesis, which I completed in 2011. It is, however, a much revised and updated version of the thesis, bettered through my increased experience since completing the thesis. Writing the thesis was tough enough – writing a book for a wider, and perhaps more critical, audience was even tougher. But my belief that the book's message was important to the future of the CDM and any new market mechanism was, for me, inspiration enough to keep at it. And I am glad I did.

Acknowledgements

There are so many people who have been a huge help to me in this project, and I might not be able to list them all here. My deep appreciation goes to all those who assisted me, gave me inspiration and encouragement, helped talk things over with me, and just supported me in many different ways.

I would like to thank my husband, Niyi, and my mum and dad for their never-ending encouragement and belief in me. You gave me the strength to see this through, so thank you. I also thank my siblings and all my family, as well as my friends, particularly those from RCCG Open Heavens Dundee, for being there for me always. To my darling son, Daniel, you are a constant source of joy to me and I love you.

My thanks also go to my PhD supervisors, Elizabeth Kirk and Andrea Ross, who, although I have graduated, have remained very supportive of me. Thank you for taking the time to review portions of my manuscript, provide your comments and encourage me to keep going for it. I would also like to thank my PhD examiners, Philippe Cullet and Robin Churchill, for taking the time to consider my thesis and for their comments, which improved the final product. To John Kilani, who took the time to read through my manuscript and write the foreword, I am very grateful.

I am also grateful to my publishers for their support. In particular, Stephen Gutierrez and Mark Sapwell were both extremely helpful throughout my time working on this manuscript.

Finally, and most importantly, my deepest gratitude and appreciation go to the Almighty God, without whom I would not be where I am today. He has been my strength and support, the reason for my success.

Part I

Introduction

1 Introduction

The Clean Development Mechanism (CDM) is widely regarded as one of the Kyoto Protocol's biggest achievements and a key part of its architecture. It was established to achieve cost-effective emission reductions and to contribute to sustainable development in developing countries. In its almost 10 years of operation, it has reduced millions of tonnes of carbon dioxide, raised billions of dollars of investment in developing countries and saved developed countries billions of dollars in compliance costs.

Nevertheless, the mechanism has several shortcomings. It has been criticised for allowing projects that will not sufficiently contribute to developing countries' sustainable development. Another key shortcoming is the poor distribution of CDM projects and their benefits among developing countries.

The first CDM project was registered in 2004, and there are now well over 6,500 registered projects, expected to reduce over 848 million tonnes of carbon dioxide annually (CDM Pipeline (http://cdmpipeline.org/), 1 March 2013). The total investment in registered projects and those undergoing registration was estimated to be about US$215.4 billion as of June 2012 (UNFCCC 2012: 42–4). There are 129 countries eligible to participate in the CDM, and 84 of these have registered projects. However, of this number, just 2 countries – China and India – host over 70 per cent of all registered projects (CDM Pipeline, 1 March 2013). These 2 countries also accounted for 65 per cent of the total investment in CDM projects as of June 2012 (UNFCCC 2012: 44). Understandably, therefore, this is a serious problem that countries have been keen to resolve.

This book focuses on this issue of equity in the geographic distribution of CDM projects among developing countries. Its aim is to identify ways to promote a more equitable distribution of CDM projects among developing countries, in order to ensure that as many countries as possible are able to enjoy the benefits of the CDM.

Specifically, this book has three main objectives. It analyses how distributive justice is achieved in international law and, using this as a basis, defines equitable distribution of CDM projects and outlines the ideal distribution of projects. It then identifies the main reasons why the distribution of CDM projects remains inequitable and all the efforts to promote equitable distribution have not achieved their goal. And, finally, it suggests measures that can be taken to ensure a more equitable distribution of CDM projects.

This book shows that, although there are many factors that contribute to the inequitable geographical distribution of CDM projects, there are two principal reasons for the continuing inequity. First, there is a dominance of unilateral CDM projects in the CDM market, which has effectively shut out those countries without the financial and technical capacity to unilaterally develop and implement projects. Second, as a result of the market-based nature of the CDM, in which cost-effectiveness, risk minimisation and profit maximisation are key, and the sustainable development contributions of CDM projects are not monetised, investors have gravitated towards the countries with the potential for low-cost, low-risk, high-profit projects. Indeed, these countries have dominated the CDM market, and other countries have been left far behind.

This book also reveals that these two principal barriers have resulted in a situation where the countries that are most in need of the benefits of the CDM, because of their low development levels, have been largely excluded from the mechanism and so are benefiting the least from it. It shows that this is because most of these countries lack the technical capacity and access to finance to undertake unilateral projects. Most of them also have small economies and lack the high emission levels and institutional capacity (and the attendant potential for low-risk, high-profit projects) that CDM investors prefer. Although, generally, these countries have great potential for projects that deliver high sustainable development benefits, this is not a particular advantage under the CDM, as the sustainable development element of the CDM, unlike its greenhouse gas (GHG) emission reduction element, has no monetary value put on it.

The book recommends that, to address these barriers, there is a need to establish a project development and implementation fund and also to regulate the CDM market by, for instance, limiting the percentage of permitted unilateral projects and mandating consideration of countries' sustainable development potential. It argues that such regulations will not substantially affect investors' interest in the CDM market, considering the size of the CDM market and the fact that the use of the CDM has saved developed countries and their entities an estimated US$3.6 billion in compliance costs.

This book begins by defining the term 'equitable distribution of CDM projects', which is a commonly used, yet undefined, reference to distributive justice in CDM parlance. This is a significant contribution because, although countries have, for years, been calling for an equitable distribution of projects and making efforts in this regard, this term has never actually been defined. Without such a definition, the goal being strived for remains unclear. As noted by the Secretariat of the United Nations Framework Convention on Climate Change (UNFCCC or Convention):

> Assessing the distribution of CDM projects requires a benchmark – an equitable regional distribution – against which the actual distribution of CDM projects can be compared. Neither the CMP [Conference of the Parties serving as the meeting of the parties to the Kyoto Protocol] nor researchers have defined 'equitable regional distribution'.
>
> (UNFCCC 2012: 61)

This book addresses this gap.

Also, as shown in Chapter 9, a lot of effort has gone into promoting an equitable distribution of projects. However, these measures have not made much difference in the distribution of projects. This book establishes the reason for this, showing that none of the measures addresses the fundamental barriers to equitable distribution, and that, until these fundamental barriers are addressed, the distribution of projects will remain inequitable.

It is important to note at this stage that the second commitment period under the Kyoto Protocol has begun and runs to 2020. This means that the CDM is now in its second operational phase. The question of whether or not there will be a third phase (that is, whether there will be a third Kyoto Protocol commitment period) is still uncertain, but unlikely. This is because countries are currently working to establish a new global agreement, which would essentially replace the Kyoto Protocol. This agreement is expected to be adopted in 2015 and come into force in 2020. When this happens, the CDM in its current form will likely 'lapse', as the Kyoto Protocol would at this point come to a natural end, although there is some expectation that, together with some of the Kyoto Protocol institutions, the CDM will continue in some form under this new agreement.

The issues addressed in this book are pertinent to the CDM in this second phase and will remain pertinent to any future market mechanism that is established under the new agreement, including the new market mechanism that was 'defined' by the seventeenth session of the Conference of the Parties (COP17) in 2011 (discussed further in Chapter 10). It is important that, in designing a new market mechanism or mechanisms, countries learn from past and current mistakes, so as to ensure that the regime is properly placed to achieve an equitable distribution of projects and their benefits.

Another important point to note is on terminology. This book focuses on distributive justice under the CDM, and, under the CDM regime, the specific term used to refer to this is 'equitable distribution'. Consequently, this book uses 'equitable distribution' when referring to the CDM, but 'distributive justice' when speaking more generally.

This book is divided into three main parts. Part I contains an introduction to the CDM, explaining what it is, as well as its objectives, operation and structure. It also contains an explanation of the need to achieve an equitable distribution of CDM projects.

The focus of Part II is on defining equitable distribution of CDM projects. It starts by analysing the framework of equity under the international climate change regime, as well as the approach to distributive justice in international law generally. It shows that generally, in international law, distributive justice is achieved through a process that takes full account of specific factors and that, by ensuring a balance among these factors, achieves an equitable or just outcome. This reflects the approach to equity taken in the climate change regime, which generally requires consideration of countries' needs, responsibility and capability, and supports this by giving certain countries preferential treatment. It concludes that, under the CDM, equitable distribution requires due consideration of countries' emission reduction potential and need (sustainable development potential), supported by preferential treatment for the countries with the greatest need. The distribution that results from full consideration of these two elements can then be regarded as equitable. Using this definition, it finds that the current distribution of projects is inequitable.

Part III undertakes a critique of the legal regime governing the CDM to identify the reasons for the inequitable distribution of projects. By analysing the challenges faced by countries in accessing the CDM, it determines that the two main barriers to equitable geographic distribution of projects are the dominance of unilateral CDM projects in the CDM market and the market nature of the CDM. Recommending regulations of the CDM market to address these barriers, this book contends that, despite reluctance to regulate the CDM because of its market nature, such regulations are necessary if the CDM is to achieve equity in its distribution of projects among developing countries.

2 The Clean Development Mechanism

> The clean development mechanism (CDM) is a unique mechanism for global collaboration that seeks to mitigate climate change while delivering sustainable development to the developing countries that host CDM projects.[1]

The CDM is a double-headed tool designed to both achieve cost-effective GHG emission reductions and deliver sustainable development. Accomplishing both objectives is vital to the success of the CDM, and understanding both is key to tackling the challenge of delivering equitable distribution of projects. This chapter begins with a brief overview of the CDM as a tool for mitigating climate change and promoting sustainable development. It explains some of the key benefits of the mechanism and outlines its structure and participation requirements.

The objectives and benefits of the CDM also explain why countries should strive to achieve an equitable geographic distribution of projects. Because both objectives of the CDM are equally important, the need to achieve an equitable distribution of projects must not be overlooked. This chapter explores the motivation for the establishment of the CDM and the expressed expectations of its proponents, highlighting that one of the main reasons for developing countries' acceptance of the CDM was the reassurance that it would contribute to their sustainable development. The concentration of most CDM projects (and the benefits they provide) in just a few developing countries is therefore very much a concern for most developing countries, and justifiably so.

---

1 Comment made by Mr Kivutha Kibwana, Minister for the Environment and Natural Resources of Kenya and President of the Conference of the Parties serving as the Meeting of the Parties to the Kyoto Protocol at its second session (COP/MOP2), when introducing the agenda item on issues relating to the CDM. See Report of COP/MOP 2 (FCCC/KP/CMP/2006/10, 26 January 2007), paragraph 31.

2.1   Overview of the CDM

The CDM is a market-based instrument of the Kyoto Protocol under which project activities that result in reduced GHG emissions can be implemented in developing countries. Such activities vary considerably – they range from small projects that replace incandescent light bulbs with compact fluorescent bulbs, to much larger projects that involve the construction of wind farms to supply renewable energy and replace fossil fuel-generated energy.

The CDM was conceived as a way of increasing direct investment into developing countries, where the cost of mitigation is much lower than in developed countries. Developing countries would benefit from this investment and the contribution it would make to their sustainable development, and developed countries could use the emission reduction credits (Certified Emission Reductions, or CERs) generated by these projects to contribute to meeting their Kyoto Protocol emission reduction commitments (Kyoto Protocol, Article 12.3).

The CDM is one of the three 'flexibility' mechanisms established under the Kyoto Protocol to give developed countries some flexibility in how they meet their Kyoto Protocol commitments and also to reduce the cost of meeting these commitments. To be registered as a CDM project, a project must show that it will result in emission reductions that are additional to any that would occur in the absence of the project (Kyoto Protocol, Article 12.5(c)). This is known as the additionality test.

To prove additionality, it is necessary to establish a baseline, which is the scenario that represents the level of GHG emissions that would ordinarily be produced in the absence of the proposed project activity. Reductions below this baseline as a result of the CDM project are the additional reductions, and it is for these that CERs are issued. One CER is equal to 1 tonne of carbon dioxide equivalent (CO_2e) reduced (such as through an energy efficiency project) or removed from the atmosphere (such as through an afforestation project) (Decision 3/CMP.1, Annex, paragraph 1).

The two main objectives of the CDM are to contribute to sustainable development in developing countries and to contribute to climate change mitigation through the GHG emission reductions achieved by projects. Generally, in relation to developing countries, the CDM aims to assist developing countries to achieve sustainable development and to contribute to the ultimate objective of the Convention. In relation to developed countries, the CDM aims to provide them with cost-effective opportunities to comply with their emission reduction commitments (Kyoto Protocol, Article 12.2).

CDM project activities implemented in developing countries represent funding and investment that are additional to the official development assistance received by these countries and are also additional to the financial obligations of developed countries contained in the Convention (Decision 17/CP.7, Preamble, paragraph 7; Decision 3/CMP.1, Appendix B, paragraph 2(f)). This investment should assist developing countries in achieving their sustainable development objectives, including their economic and environmental goals, by, for example, providing clean technology, access to energy, more jobs, capacity building, and cleaner air and water, and ensuring more sustainable use of land and other natural resources. The benefit to developed countries is the lower marginal abatement cost of reducing emissions in developing countries compared with reducing them in developed countries. For instance, it is estimated that the CDM has saved developed countries and their entities about US$3.6 billion in compliance costs (UNFCCC 2012: 58–9).

The Kyoto Protocol is now in its second commitment period, and the CDM is therefore in its second operational phase, running from 1 January 2013 to 31 December 2020 (Decision 1/CMP.8, paragraph 4). Countries are currently negotiating a new global agreement, which is expected to come into force and be implemented from 2020 (Decision 2/CP.18, paragraph 4). This is discussed in a bit more detail in Chapter 10.

2.1.1 CDM participation requirements

The legal regime governing the CDM lays down certain participation requirements, and only those countries that fulfil these requirements can participate in the CDM. There are three basic requirements that must be fulfilled by both developed and developing countries to make them eligible to participate in the CDM. These requirements are: ratification of the Kyoto Protocol, establishment of a designated national authority (DNA) and (confirmation of) voluntary participation:

(a) Ratification of the Kyoto Protocol: participation in the CDM is only open to those countries that have ratified the Protocol, and therefore countries may only participate in the CDM once they become parties to the Protocol (Decision 3/CMP.1, Annex, paragraphs 30 and 31(a)). Both private entities, such as companies, and public entities, such as governments or government agencies, are allowed to participate in the CDM (Kyoto Protocol, Article 12.9). However, before private entities can participate in the CDM, they must be authorised to do so by eligible countries (Decision 3/CMP.1, Annex, paragraph 33). In addition, developed countries must also accept the Doha Amendment to the Kyoto Protocol and take on second commitment period targets, to be eligible to fully participate in the CDM in the second commitment period (Decision 1/CMP.8, paragraphs 13–14).

As of April 2013, there are 152 developing country parties to the Kyoto Protocol. Afghanistan ratified the Protocol in March 2013, and the Protocol will enter into force for it in June 2013.[2]

2 See 'Parties to the Convention and Observer States'. Online. Available at: http://unfccc. int/parties_and_observers/parties/items/2352.php. 'Status of ratification of the Kyoto Protocol'. Online. Available at: http://unfccc.int/kyoto_protocol/status_of_ratification/ items/2613.php (accessed 30 April 2013).

(b) Establishment of a DNA: to participate in the CDM, countries must establish a DNA for the CDM (Decision 3/CMP.1, Annex, paragraph 29), which will serve as a point of contact within that country for information on the CDM (UNDP 2003: 60–2). The DNAs of parties are listed on the CDM website.[3]

The functions of the DNA are primarily to communicate voluntary participation in the CDM and, in the case of the host country DNA, to confirm that the CDM project activity will assist the host country in achieving its sustainable development goals (Decision 3/CMP.1, Annex, paragraph 40(a)). As of April 2013, 129 developing countries have established DNAs. This means 129 developing countries are eligible to participate in the CDM (Appendix A). Although there are three participation requirements, in practical terms, eligibility is determined by the first two (Kyoto Protocol ratification and DNA establishment). Countries must then approve their participation in each project activity, to signify their voluntary participation, as discussed below.

(c) Voluntary participation: participation in the CDM is voluntary. Hence, countries must approve their participation in each project activity (Kyoto Protocol, Article 12.5(a); Decision 3/CMP.1, Annex, paragraph 28). The project participants involved in each project must provide written notice confirming that they are participating voluntarily in the project (Decision 3/CMP.1, Annex, paragraph 40(a)). Participants obtain this written notice from their country DNA, whose responsibility it is to provide notice of voluntary participation (Decision 3/CMP.1, Annex, paragraph 40(a)).

2.1.2 *Structure of the CDM*

Article 12 of the Kyoto Protocol defines the CDM as a mechanism under which developing countries benefit from project activities resulting in CERs, and developed countries can use the CERs generated from such project activities to comply with part of their emission reduction targets. This definition of the CDM is somewhat vague and does not specify its exact structure, other than that it is to be project-based. However, as the rules and practice have been established and/or developed, the structure of the CDM has emerged, showing three elements: it is project- and market-based and has an 'open architecture'.

The CDM operates at the project level. Under the CDM, individual project activities are registered (after undergoing the registration process) and can then generate CERs, which developed countries can use for the purpose of

---

3 'Full list of DNAs.' Online. Available at: http://cdm.unfccc.int/DNA/bak/index.html (accessed 30 April 2013).

meeting their Protocol targets (Kyoto Protocol, Article 12.3; Lecocq and Ambrosi 2007: 139). In addition to the registration of individual project activities as single CDM projects, several project activities can be registered as a single CDM project under the CDM Programme of Activities (CDM PoA).

The CDM Executive Board has defined a CDM PoA as a coordinated action by a public or private entity that coordinates and implements any policy/measure or stated goal, such as incentive schemes. Such a policy/measure or goal must be voluntary, that is, not mandated by the law of the host country. It can be implemented via an unlimited number of project activities (referred to as component project activities, or CPAs), which must result in GHG emission reductions or removals that are additional to any that would occur in the absence of the activities.[4] CPAs can be included in the PoA at the time of registration, and an unlimited number can be added to the PoA at any time in the duration of the PoA. These activities can take place in a single or multiple locations and can involve a single measure or interrelated measures to reduce GHG emissions (UNEP 2009: 11).

The CDM is also a market-based instrument under which developed country entities can either invest in GHG emission reduction projects in developing countries and benefit from the CERs generated, or buy CERs directly from host developing countries or entities, or other developed country entities (UNDP 2003: 11). The CDM has created a market in which private entities play a major role, and in which CERs can be bought and sold at prices largely determined by market forces (Lecocq and Ambrosi 2007: 139–40; Kossoy and Guigon 2012). Chapter 8 discusses the CDM as a market mechanism in greater detail.

Third, the CDM can be described as having an 'open architecture', in which unilateral, bilateral and multilateral CDM projects are allowed (Baumert *et al.* 2000). Unilateral projects are projects developed, financed and implemented by host developing country entities, which then sell on the CERs generated by the projects. Here, there is no foreign investment, and developed country entities would simply buy CERs from the host developing country entities. Bilateral projects involve developed country entities in the development, financing and implementation of the projects. These projects involve foreign investment in the actual CDM projects, beyond mere purchase of the CERs generated by the projects.

Multilateral projects involve several developed country public or private entities, which usually act through (multilateral) funds. The developed country entities, which are interested in obtaining CERs, contribute money

---

4   See 'Procedures for registration of a programme of activities as a single CDM project activity and issuance of certified emission reductions for a programme of activities' (version 03), Report of the 47th Meeting of the Executive Board, Annex 29 (May 2009) http://cdm.unfccc.int/EB/047/eb47_repan29.pdf (accessed 30 April 2013), 1.

to these funds, and the funds then invest in projects or purchase CERs on behalf of the contributing entities. Examples include the various carbon funds administered by the World Bank, such as the Prototype Carbon Fund, which is a partnership of seventeen companies and six governments.[5] In this scenario, the funds either invest directly in the underlying project, as with bilateral projects, or merely purchase the CERs generated, as with unilateral projects. The difference is that, in the multilateral structure, the fund acts on behalf of several developed country entities, the funding provided by the developed country entities is channelled through this fund, and the CERs generated are for the benefit of these entities. All three models currently operate in the CDM market.

2.2 The need for equitable geographic distribution

Part of the rationale behind the establishment of the CDM was that emission reductions achieved in developing countries are as beneficial to the atmosphere as emission reductions achieved in developed countries. In taking advantage of the lower cost of reducing emissions in developing countries, developed countries would be doing as much good to the atmosphere as if they were reducing the emissions in their own countries. Therefore, as it does not actually matter to the atmosphere where emission reductions take place, it could be suggested that it does not matter where CDM projects are hosted, provided CDM projects are being registered, and climate change mitigation is being achieved. There are currently 6,556 registered CDM projects and over 2,000 more in the pipeline, but the distribution of these projects among developing countries varies considerably, from many countries hosting no project at all, to a few hosting several hundred projects, and one country (China) hosting several thousand (CDM Pipeline, 1 March 2013). This might appear to some as a perfectly acceptable situation.

However, one of the main reasons for seeking equitable geographic distribution of projects lies in the CDM's objective of promoting sustainable development. The Kyoto Protocol states that the CDM should, inter alia, contribute to sustainable development in developing countries (Kyoto Protocol, Article 12.2). The CDM is not intended to contribute to the sustainable development of just a few developing countries, but of as many countries as possible.

A key driver of developing countries' acceptance of the CDM during the Kyoto Protocol negotiations was the explicit mention of sustainable development as a goal of the CDM. They accepted the mechanism with the

5   See 'Prototype Carbon Fund'. Online. Available at: http://web.worldbank.org/WBSITE/ EXTERNAL/TOPICS/ENVIRONMENT/EXTCARBONFINANCE/0,,contentMDK:21630 008~menuPK:5216148~pagePK:64168445~piPK:64168309~theSitePK:4125853,00.html (accessed 30 April 2013).

expectation that it would help them achieve sustainable development – it was never the intention that it would only benefit a select few countries (Huq 2002: 22; Michaelowa 2005). The Chairman of the African Group to COP 12 is quoted as saying, 'If we knew then what we know now, we would not have agreed to the CDM', referring to the fact that the CDM is not working for Africa (Oppenoorth *et al.* 2007: 17).

According to the Convention, countries have a right to promote sustainable development (UNFCCC, Article 3.4), and one of the central principles of sustainable development is equity, including in the distribution of resources, in order to eradicate poverty and ensure the meeting of (basic) needs (ILA 2002: 213 (principle 2.1); Segger and Khalfan 2004: 122–32; French 2005: 28–30, 59–62, 65–6). In addition to ensuring the meeting of needs and eradication of poverty, the other key component of sustainable development is the protection of the environment – sustainable development aims at ensuring that economic development and environmental protection are achieved in an integrated manner.

Equitable geographic distribution of CDM projects will provide all developing countries with the opportunity to do both – to enjoy the social and economic benefits of CDM projects, and also to protect the environment through the GHG emission reductions achieved by projects.[6] As highlighted above, the CDM provides a range of benefits to the host developing countries, including access to energy, job creation and technology. The total investment in CDM projects in the pipeline (registered and soon-to-be-registered projects) is estimated to be about US$215.4 billion as of June 2012. The average investment per project is approximately US$45 million (UNFCCC 2012: 42–4). These are some of the benefits that countries thought they would all share in equitably. However, China and India alone account for 65 per cent of this investment (UNFCCC 2012: 44). This is clearly a cause for concern.

Therefore, because the CDM is a mechanism for achieving GHG emission reductions and for promoting sustainable development, to ensure that all developing countries are able to take advantage of CDM projects and the benefits they provide, the location and distribution of projects *are* important.

Countries recognise this need for equitable distribution of projects and have repeatedly called for this, making it obvious that it is, in fact, important to them. In 2001, when establishing the rules to govern the CDM, COP 7 recognised the need to promote equitable distribution of projects (Decision 17/CP.7, Preamble, paragraph 6). Subsequently, at COP/MOP 1

6   Article 12 of the Protocol provides that, in relation to developing countries, the objectives of the CDM are to help these countries achieve sustainable development and also to contribute to the Convention's ultimate objective of stabilising GHG concentrations in the atmosphere.

in December 2005 identified addressing the issue of equitable distribution of CDM projects as one of its roles, with a focus on the regional and sub-regional distribution of projects (Decision 3/CMP.1, Annex, paragraph 4(c)). At COP/MOP 2, the CDM Executive Board reported on its efforts to promote equitable distribution, such as the adoption of simplified modalities for small-scale projects and establishment of the DNA Forum (EB 2006: paragraph 9). All subsequent decisions in relation to the CDM acknowledge the need to ensure an equitable distribution of CDM projects among countries and regions, and various actions have been taken, all aimed at achieving this goal.

In addition, the UNFCCC and its Kyoto Protocol have equity as one of the key principles of the climate change regime. Equity is factored into every aspect of the climate change regime, from the ultimate objective of the regime, to the activities to achieve this objective (such as in the distribution of the responsibilities for addressing the climate change problem), and the financing of these activities. This is discussed in more detail in Chapter 3. As an instrument of this regime, the CDM first must follow these principles and rules and, second, was established, among other things, to contribute to the fulfilment of the objectives of the regime. It is therefore important that the CDM, like the Convention and Protocol, should promote equity in its implementation, including in the way CDM projects, which are the main products of the CDM, are distributed.

Unfortunately, this goal has proven elusive, and the distribution of CDM projects, both nationally and regionally, is still inequitable. It is important to determine why, in order to help fulfil both objectives of the mechanism, as well as to ensure equity among developing countries. However, before ascertaining the reasons for the inequitable distribution of projects, it is necessary first to determine the meaning of equitable distribution of projects, so as to identify what an equitable distribution should look like. Despite their repeated calls for an equitable distribution of projects, countries have not defined or described the meaning of the term 'equitable geographic distribution', neither has the ideal distribution of projects among countries been identified. It is on this that Part II focuses.

Part II

Defining equitable distribution

Part II, which comprises Chapters 3–6, focuses on defining the term 'equitable distribution of CDM projects'. This definition is one of the major contributions of this book, as the lack of a definition means that the goal that countries are striving for is uncertain, and that achievement or otherwise of the goal cannot be measured. This part does both. It defines equitable distribution and also ascertains whether the current distribution of projects is equitable.

Before embarking on the process of identifying a suitable definition of equitable distribution, it is important to identify the parameters of the process: any definition of equitable distribution must be appropriate for the CDM and support it in achieving its objectives of contributing to GHG emissions reduction and sustainable development. This book resists the temptation to simply select an approach to equity, without determining its suitability for achieving the objectives of the CDM.

This part uses as a starting point the approach to equity under the international climate change regime (the regime under which the CDM operates) and distributive justice in international law. Using this foundation and the objectives of the CDM, it determines the meaning of equitable distribution (distributive justice) under the CDM and the factors to be considered in efforts to achieve such a distribution. Finally, this part provides a general outline of how CDM projects should be distributed and, comparing the current distribution to this outline, concludes that the current distribution of projects under the CDM is inequitable.

3 Equity under the international climate change regime

Equity is one of the fundamental principles of the international climate change regime. This regime, which consists primarily of the UNFCCC and the Kyoto Protocol, has equity factored into every aspect, from its ultimate objective (UNFCCC, Article 2), to the activities to achieve this objective,[1] the financing of these activities (UNFCCC, Article 4.7) and participation in governance.[2] This chapter examines the international climate change regime and its framework of equity, in order to provide some context and guidance for the application of equity under the CDM.

Speaking about equity in the regime, it is important to note, first, that the problem of climate change itself raises issues of equity, particularly with regard to the causes and impacts of the problem. This is because those who have contributed the least to climate change face most of its impacts. Climate change is historically attributable to the developed world, but developing countries, which have historically contributed the least to climate change, are expected to be the most affected by it (McCarthy *et al.* 2001: 8).

In addition to the fact that developing countries will suffer the worst effects of climate change, generally, they also have the least capacity to adapt to these effects.[3] Developed countries, with their greater resources and technological advancement, are generally recognised as having a greater

1 The Convention and Protocol contain differentiated commitments for different groups of countries on the basis of equity.
2 For example, the COP presidency rotates among the five UN regional groupings, and the COP Bureau consists of eleven members – two each from the five regional groupings and one from SIDS. See the Draft Rules of Procedure of the Conference of the Parties and its Subsidiary Bodies (FCCC/CP/1996/2), Rule 22(1). Additionally, it is practice to have one member from a developed country and one from a developing country to be the chair and vice-chair of the various subsidiary bodies under the Convention. Also, when establishing contact groups during negotiating sessions, the contact groups are usually co-chaired by a representative each from a developed and developing country party.
3 There are, of course, exceptions to this statement – many countries regarded as 'developing countries' are actually quite wealthy, such as Qatar and Barbados.

capacity to address climate change than developing countries, through, for instance, the development of low-carbon technologies.

The issue of historical responsibility for climate change also raises another issue of equity. Developing countries point out that developed countries have had many years to develop and, in this process, have caused the current climate change problem. They argue that they (developing countries) in turn need to increase their energy use in order to achieve development and alleviate poverty in their countries (Pittock 2005: 216). The Convention recognises that, in order to achieve sustainable social and economic development, developing countries need access to resources, and that their energy consumption will grow, albeit taking account of the possibilities for achieving greater energy efficiency and for controlling GHG emissions (UNFCCC, Preamble, paragraph 22).

This is one of the reasons why developing countries have resisted attempts to cap their GHG emissions, as they fear this would likewise cap their development. Responsible development, however, means that this should not be taken to mean unrestricted freedom to continue to produce GHG emissions. Any consumption that leads to GHG emissions should be done in light of the need for 'sustainable' development. Economic development, which for developing countries means increasing economic growth, should be achieved sustainably, in a manner that considers the need to protect the environment and preserve the ability of others, both in the present and the future, to meet their own needs.

These inequities are part of the main drivers of the international climate change regime. They are the reason why equity is built into the design of the regime, and efforts were made to ensure that those who contributed least to the problem do not take on disproportionate responsibilities to solve it (UNFCCC, Preamble, paragraphs 3, 19 and 20; and Article 3.1).

The Convention establishes several guiding principles for the implementation of the climate change regime (UNFCCC, Article 3.1). Of these principles, those that relate to equity within the regime are:

- protection of the climate for the benefit of present and future generations of humankind on the basis of equity;
- the principle of common but differentiated responsibilities and respective capabilities, which also includes the requirement for developed countries to take the lead in combating climate change and its adverse effects and the requirement that the specific needs and special circumstances of developing countries should be given full consideration; and
- the importance of sustainable development and sustainable economic growth, and the right to promote sustainable development.

These principles are examined in greater detail on pp. 19–23.

3.1 Protecting the climate for current and future generations on the basis of equity

The Convention provides that parties should protect the climate system for the benefit of present and future generations of humankind, on the basis of equity (UNFCCC, Article 3.1). This provision of the climate change regime relates to the principles of intra- and inter-generational equity. Under international law, these principles aim to ensure fairness among individuals and countries in the present and future generations (Shelton 2007: 642). They are key principles of sustainable development, which is also one of the stated aims of the CDM.

Intra-generational equity aims for justice among members of the present generation and requires fairness in the use of resources, both nationally and internationally (Maggio 1996–7: 161, 163–164). It also includes considerations of distribution of resources and justice between and within nations (Segger and Khalfan 2004: 125). Inter-generational equity is based on the idea that the present generation holds the earth in trust for future generations. It should therefore use the earth's resources 'fairly' to meet its needs, so that future generations have enough resources to meet their own needs (Maggio 1996–7: 163; Shelton 2007: 642). For this reason, the Rio Declaration on Environment and Development provides that 'the right to development must be fulfilled so as to equitably meet developmental and environmental needs of present and future generations' (Rio Declaration, Principle 4).

Under the climate change regime, application of the principle can be seen in provisions requiring countries to take necessary action to protect the climate in order to ensure that present and future generations can meet their needs. For example, the Convention calls for urgent action to prevent dangerous interference with the climate system, in consideration of the needs of future generations. It also requires developed countries to take the lead in this 'urgent action', in consideration of the needs of the present generation, because, inter alia, the share of global emissions originating in developing countries will need to grow to meet their social and development needs (UNFCCC, Article 3.1 and Preamble, paragraph 3).

It is apparent from the above that, for both intra- and inter-generational equity, a major concern is the meeting of the needs of others: equity requires generations to utilise resources in such a way as to ensure that others within that generation (intra-generational equity) or in future generations (inter-generational equity) are able to meet their own needs. In this regard, the needs of others, and meeting these needs, are of paramount importance. These principles also highlight global interconnectedness – no human or country is an island, as the popular saying goes. Even those that geographically are islands are not, when regarded economically or materially. These principles place emphasis on the need to consider the impacts of one's action (or inaction) on others.

In relation to the CDM, this suggests that consideration of the needs of countries should form part of efforts to ensure equity in the distribution of projects. Particularly if taken to refer to countries' need for sustainable development, this element of 'needs' *is* relevant to the distribution of CDM projects. This is discussed in greater detail in Chapter 5.

3.2 Common but differentiated responsibilities and respective capabilities

The principle of common but differentiated responsibilities and respective capabilities (CBDR) is one that is commonly applied under international environmental law. Many multilateral environmental agreements incorporate this principle with the aim of ensuring equity within the regimes (Cullet 1999: 169; Sands 2003: 285–9), and the Rio Declaration highlights its connection to the pursuit of sustainable development (Rio Declaration, Principle 7). For instance, the principle can be seen in the Montreal Protocol, the International Tropical Timber Agreement and the Convention on Biological Diversity (Montreal Protocol, Article 5; International Tropical Timber Agreement, Article 34; Convention on Biological Diversity, Preamble, paragraph 17).

It is also a key principle in the climate regime, and one that is often evoked during negotiations (Cazorla and Toman 2000: 1–3).[4] The principle has two essential elements: countries' common responsibility to protect the climate; and countries' differentiated responsibilities, based on their contribution to the problem and capacity to address it. It recognises that climate change is the common concern of all countries, and that they should all participate in international efforts to address the problem. The Convention therefore contains general commitments for all countries to fulfil (UNFCCC, Article 4.1).

The principle, however, also recognises that there are differences in countries' contributions to climate change (and, generally, other forms of environmental degradation) and in their financial and technical capacity to address it, and that there must, therefore, be differences in their responsibility to address it. There is general acceptance that developed countries have contributed the most to climate change (UNFCCC, Preamble, paragraph 3).[5] In addition, these countries, because of their greater wealth

---

4   See also the *Earth Negotiations Bulletin* reports of the climate change negotiations. Online. Available at: www.iisd.ca/process/climate_atm.htm#climate (accessed 30 April 2013).

5   Although it is generally agreed that developed countries are historically responsible for the current level of GHG emissions in the atmosphere, developing country emissions are predicted to exceed developed country emissions in the future, and, in fact, some developing country emissions already exceed those of many developed countries.

and technological advancement, are better able to address climate change – they have greater capabilities. Therefore, according to the Convention, 'the developed country parties should take the lead in combating climate change and the adverse effects thereof' (UNFCCC, Article 3.1).

Consequently, the Convention contains additional commitments for developed countries in light of their historical responsibility (UNFCCC, Article 4). The Protocol also contains commitments regarding policies and measures, GHG emission reductions and reporting for developed countries, with no corresponding commitments for developing countries (Kyoto Protocol, Articles 2, 3, 5 and 7). There is also differentiation among developed countries, with those countries that are making the transition to a market economy being exempt from some of the financial obligations that other developed countries have, in recognition of their lesser financial capability (UNFCCC, Article 4.3).

In allocating differentiated responsibilities, the CBDR principle achieves equity by granting preferential treatment to certain groups of countries. Such preferential treatment is often expressed as a requirement to take account of the special circumstances, needs or requirements of specific groups. This requirement is not unique to the climate change regime – many international agreements incorporate some form of it in efforts to ensure equity in the treatment of specific groups of countries, usually developing countries (UNCLOS, Preamble, paragraph 5; Vienna Convention, Preamble, paragraph 3; 1976 Barcelona Convention, Article 11.3; Montreal Protocol, Article 5; and Convention on Biological Diversity, Preamble, paragraph 17). The UN Millennium Declaration recognises the obstacles faced by developing countries in mobilising the resources needed to finance their sustained development, as well as the special needs and problems of small-island developing States (SIDS) and the least developed countries (LDCs) (UN Millennium Declaration, Section III).

As applied under the climate change regime, this principle requires consideration of developing countries' specific needs and special circumstances, such as their right to promote sustainable development (UNFCCC, Article 3.4), their need to achieve sustained economic growth and eradicate poverty (UNFCCC, Preamble, paragraph 21 and Article 4.7), as well as their need for support with climate change education and training, and capacity building (Kyoto Protocol, Article 10(e); Decision 11/CP.8). The Protocol urges developed countries to implement policies and measures in such a way as to minimise adverse effects on other countries, especially developing countries (Kyoto Protocol, Article 2.3). It is also applied through the requirement for international assistance, including financial aid and technology transfer, usually to developing countries (French 2000: 42; Rajamani 2006: 107–14).

These general provisions can also be used to distinguish between the needs of individual developing countries, rather than between developed and developing countries. For instance, the Convention explicitly recognises certain groups of developing countries as having special circumstances that should be considered. These include the LDCs, as well as those developing countries that are particularly vulnerable to the adverse effects of climate change and/or the impact of the implementation of response measures (UNFCCC, Preamble, paragraph 19, and Articles 4.8, 4.9 and 4.10).

The CDM itself is a key differentiation mechanism under the climate change regime. In recognition of their limited responsibility for the climate problem and their limited capability to address it, developing countries do not have emission reduction commitments under the Kyoto Protocol. However, through the CDM, they are given the chance to contribute to climate change mitigation. In addition, in recognition of their need for sustainable development, CDM projects are required to contribute to sustainable development in developing countries.

In conclusion, the CBDR principle advocates different obligations to address a problem, based on responsibility for (or contribution to) the problem, capability to address it and needs. It also supports giving preferential treatment based on these elements. It is important to note, however, that the principle is not meant to be static, but dynamic, considering the situation and circumstances of countries at the relevant point in time, not just at the time the Convention was agreed (Halvorssen 2007: 258–60; Guruswamy 1999–2000: 343 and 363).

3.3 Right to promote sustainable development

The right to development is often linked to equity and is applied to ensure equal and adequate access to essential resources (Sengupta 2002: 846 and 850; 1986 Declaration on the Right to Development, Article 8). It is also regarded as an element of sustainable development (Loibl 2004: 98; Boyle and Freestone 1999: 11–12).

This right is recognised by several international declarations (Copenhagen Declaration on Social Development, paragraphs 26(j) and 29(f); Vienna Declaration and Programme of Action, Article 10; UN Declaration on the Rights of Indigenous Peoples, Article 2.3); the Rio Declaration provides that the right to development must be fulfilled so as to equitably meet the developmental and environmental needs of present and future generations (Rio Declaration, Principle 3). No international treaty explicitly contains the 'right to development', and the UNFCCC comes closest, by explicitly asserting the right to 'promote sustainable development'.

The Convention provides that countries have a right to, and should, promote sustainable development. It further provides that countries should promote sustainable economic growth and development in all countries, especially developing countries (UNFCCC, Articles 3.4 and 3.5). These are two interrelated Convention principles aimed at protecting the right of countries to strive for sustainable economic growth and development.

These principles have been implemented under the climate change regime in several ways. It requires all countries, including developing countries, to protect the climate by, for instance, formulating and implementing climate change mitigation measures (UNFCCC, Article 4.1(b)). It, however, gives developing countries far fewer commitments and obligations than developed countries, in recognition of the fact that they (developing countries) have greater needs and fewer resources. It recognises their need for poverty eradication, increased energy resources, technology transfer and financial support, among others (UNFCCC, Preamble, paragraph 21, and Articles 4.3, 4.5 and 4.7), while, at the same time, requiring them to consider the possibilities for achieving greater energy efficiency and controlling GHG emissions (UNFCCC, Preamble, paragraph 22). In addition, the regime makes provision for meeting these needs in developing countries, such as by requiring transfer of environmentally sound technology and know-how, enabling capacity building and providing financial assistance to them (UNFCCC, Articles 4.5 and 4.7; Kyoto Protocol, Article 11.2(b).

The purpose of these provisions is to help developing countries achieve social and economic development at the same time as they protect the environment and mitigate climate change, which is the objective of sustainable development. The CDM is also one of the tools employed by the climate change regime to promote sustainable development in developing countries – the mechanism aims to support developing countries, in recognition of their greater needs and lesser capacity, to achieve economic development and climate change mitigation in an integrated manner.

Equity under this principle therefore has two elements: recognition and consideration of the needs of countries, and provision of support to specific groups of countries. In relation to the CDM, the element of needs and provision of support (or preferential treatment) have already been discussed under the CBDR principle. Their relevance to achieving equitable distribution under the CDM is discussed in Chapter 5.

3.4 Conclusion

This chapter has examined how the international climate change regime approaches equity. It shows that, under the regime, equity requires consideration of countries' responsibility, capability and needs. In addition, consideration of countries' needs is often manifested by the giving of preferential treatment or support (financial, technological and capacity-building support) to specific groups of countries. The climate change regime does not necessarily identify what an equitable outcome will look like – it simply establishes what should be considered in order to ensure an equitable outcome. The outcome will, therefore, vary depending on the elements and issues being considered.

For instance, because of their greater responsibility for the climate change problem, developed countries are required to take the lead in mitigating climate change and have quantified emission reduction commitments, whereas developing countries generally have no such commitments (UNFCCC, Articles

3.1 and 10; Kyoto Protocol, Annex B). In consideration of developing countries' needs and (lack of) responsibility, they have far fewer commitments than developed countries and are supposed to receive financial and technological support from developed countries to implement the commitments that they do have (UNFCCC, Article 4.7; Kyoto Protocol, Article 10). These outcomes are equitable in the context in which they were made, because of the elements that were considered in those circumstances.

It is useful to note that, if these elements were properly taken into consideration under the climate change regime today, the outcome would be different from the above outcome. 'Developing countries' are not one homogenous group with identical responsibility, needs and capability. Instead, these elements differ from country to country. Some countries considered as 'developing countries' have far greater responsibility for climate change than others, owing to their contribution to global GHG emissions. 'Developing countries' also vary widely in terms of their needs and capability – some have far fewer needs and less capability than others, owing to their low development levels. All these elements should be considered for each country, and their commitments should be defined as an output of this process. This outcome will then be truly 'equitable'.

These elements should also apply, to the extent possible, to the CDM, which is an instrument of the regime and therefore must be implemented according to the principles and rules of the regime. As already noted, the CDM itself embodies these elements of equity, as it is based on recognition of developing countries' limited responsibility for climate change and ability to address it, together with their need for sustainable development. This is discussed in greater detail in Chapter 5.

4 International law's approach to distributive justice

The pursuit of distributive justice can be seen in several international regimes. These regimes have devised means of ensuring that they are able to achieve equity in the distribution of a resource or benefit and, in doing so, have provided themselves with guidelines for achieving this. It is on these means and guidelines that this chapter focuses, examining how various international regimes achieve distributive justice. The expectation is that this will contribute to the understanding of the meaning of equitable distribution under the CDM.

The regimes examined are the delimitation of maritime boundaries under the law of the sea regime, the deep seabed regime, the fisheries regime and the international watercourses regime. These regimes are examined because they aim to achieve equity in the distribution of a benefit or resource. However, the examination shows that, because the distribution of resources is yet to commence under the deep seabed regime, and the rules for such distribution have not yet been established, there are limited lessons to be learned from this regime. The fisheries regime also offers few relevant lessons, because it has not adopted a general approach to distributive justice, nor does it regulate the distribution of fisheries resources at the international level. The international watercourses regime and maritime boundary delimitation, on the other hand, do offer some useful lessons for the CDM. These regimes are examined below.

4.1 Delimitation of maritime boundaries

This relates to the delimitation or determination of international boundaries for maritime zones, in particular, the territorial sea, the exclusive economic zone (EEZ)[1] and the continental shelf. Here, there are competing claims that

---

1 The EEZ is an area beyond and adjacent to the territorial sea and extends to a maximum of 200 nautical miles from the baselines from which the breadth of the territorial sea is measured. Within the EEZ, the coastal State enjoys extensive rights in relation to natural resources and related to jurisdictional rights, and third nations enjoy the freedom of

give rise to the need to delimit or determine maritime boundaries, which happens specifically in situations where states' maritime zones overlap because of close geographic proximity (Churchill and Lowe 1999: 181).

With regard to this aspect of the law of the sea, the courts and tribunals have said that, in delimiting maritime boundaries, they are not involved in the sharing out of something held in undivided shares, or in 'awarding a just and equitable share of a previously undelimited area' (*North Sea Continental Shelf* cases 1969: 22; *Denmark v Norway* 1993: 66–7; *Libya v Malta* 1985: 40). By this, they mean that they are not engaged in an exercise of distributive justice, drawing a distinction between delimitation and apportionment, the former being what they are engaged in (Oude Elferink 1994). Nevertheless, some of the rules or principles applied in this area could be useful in this research. For example, according to Ahnish, the aim of the law on delimitation has always been to establish principles and rules that ensure an equitable delimitation in accordance with the geography of the area concerned (Ahnish 1994: 31; Churchill and Lowe 1999: 183). Many of the provisions relating to delimitation, which will be examined below, refer to the ultimate aim of reaching an equitable outcome. For example, in the Guinea/Guinea-Bissau Arbitration (1986), the tribunal stated that all delimitations had to be measured against the single goal of reaching an equitable solution in the circumstances of the case. The International Court of Justice (ICJ or the Court) in *Romania v Ukraine* (2009: 100) pointed out that the object of delimitation is to achieve a delimitation that is equitable.

The focus here is on delimitation by courts and tribunals, when the relevant countries have been unable to reach an agreement regarding how to delimit their overlapping maritime zones. This is because countries are, of course, free to negotiate to reach agreement on delimitation, and such agreements do not necessarily have to follow the rules of the courts and tribunals, and could, for example, be based on politically motivated compromises. For example, with regard to delimitation of the territorial sea, the United Nations Convention on the Law of the Sea (UNCLOS) provides the rule that should apply in the absence of an agreement to the contrary, and, for the continental shelf, that delimitation shall be effected by agreement on the basis of international law (UNCLOS, Articles 15 and 83.1).

Regarding *the territorial sea*, the limit of the breadth of the territorial sea is 12 nautical miles from the baseline of the coastal State, which has the right to establish the breadth of its territorial sea up to this limit (UNCLOS, Article 3). Even for countries that are not party to UNCLOS, the 12-mile limit has been established in international law (Churchill and Lowe 1999: 80). Where there is a need to delimit the territorial seas of two countries,

---

navigation, overflight by aircraft and the laying of cables and pipelines. See UNCLOS, Articles 55 and 57.

where they overlap for example, the general rule is the equidistance–special circumstances rule (Churchill and Lowe 1999: 182–3). The Territorial Sea Convention and UNCLOS prohibit countries, in the absence of agreement to the contrary, from extending their territorial seas beyond the 'median line every point of which is equidistant from the nearest points on the baselines' (1958 Territorial Sea Convention, Article 12; UNCLOS, Article 15). These treaties then provide further that this rule does not apply where it is necessary by reason of special circumstances, such as historic title, to delimit the territorial seas in a different way. The equidistance–special circumstances rule is now regarded as part of customary law and is applicable to those countries not party to either the Territorial Sea Convention or UNCLOS. For example, in *Qatar v Bahrain* (2001: 94), the ICJ, noting that this equidistance–special circumstances rule is found in both the 1958 Territorial Sea Convention and UNCLOS, stated that the rule 'is to be regarded as having a customary character'. This was reflected in *Nicaragua v Honduras* (2007).

The special circumstances to be considered could include circumstances such as historic use, the presence of offshore islands, past conduct of the parties in the area, interests of third states and exceptional coastal configurations (*Beagle Channel Arbitration* 1978; *Nicaragua v Honduras* 2007: 89; University of Cambridge, *International Boundary Cases* 1992: 46–7; Ahnish 1994: Chapter 2). For example, in the *Beagle Channel Arbitration* (1978), the Arbitral Tribunal considered coastal configuration and convenience.

These circumstances generally deal with practical or geographical circumstances and are, therefore, not applicable or relevant to the issue of equitable geographic distribution of CDM projects. However, the general idea is still relevant. If the equidistance–special circumstances rule were to be applied to the CDM and equitable geographic distribution, this would mean that the distribution of CDM projects among countries should be equal or as equal as possible, except where special circumstances require otherwise. The special circumstances could include the fact that countries have different levels of GHG emissions and, therefore, cannot host the same number of projects. This is discussed further in Chapter 5. Applying this rule would result in a more equitable outcome than the current situation, where one country hosts over 3,000 projects, and many countries host none at all. Beyond this, however, the rules concerning the delimitation of the territorial sea are not directly applicable to the CDM.

With regard to *the continental shelf*, the customary law is discussed in decisions of the ICJ and arbitral tribunals. Most of the cases decided by these have in common the reference to equitable principles or an equitable basis. In the *North Sea Continental Shelf* cases (1969: 53), the ICJ held that the principles and rules of international law applicable to the delimitation of the continental shelf as between the parties included delimitation 'by agreement in accordance with equitable principles, and taking account of all the relevant circumstances'. In the *Jan Mayen* case (1993: 59), the ICJ, referring to the provisions of Articles 73 and 84 of UNCLOS on achieving an 'equitable solution', said, 'that statement of an "equitable solution" as the aim of any delimitation process reflects the requirements of customary law as regards the delimitation both of continental shelf and of exclusive economic zones'. The Court of Arbitration in the *Anglo-French* arbitration (1977) refers to the equidistance–special circumstances rule as giving expression to a general norm that, failing agreement, determination of the continental shelf should be on equitable principles (Kwiatkowska 2001: 289; Dundua 2006–7: 32, 53–82).

The rule under the 1958 Continental Shelf Convention (Article 6) is that the boundary of the continental shelf should be determined by agreement between the concerned States, but, in the absence of this and unless otherwise justified by special circumstances, the boundary was to be determined by applying the equidistance principle. This reference to special circumstances was in recognition of the fact that, in some situations, application of the equidistance principle would result in an inequitable outcome (*Anglo-French* arbitration 1977: 45; Churchill and Lowe 1999: 184). The rule under UNCLOS (Article 83.1) is that delimitation should be done by agreement on the basis of international law, in order to achieve an equitable solution. Countries are therefore encouraged to negotiate an agreement that is equitable. In making this provision, UNCLOS does not identify how parties should reach an equitable solution, or what should be taken into consideration. However, the courts have held that the rule is the 'equitable principles/relevant circumstances' rule, which according to the courts, is very similar to the 'equidistance/special circumstances' rule.

In applying this rule, the courts usually (although not necessarily) start by drawing an equidistance line and then consider whether there are factors requiring adjustment of the line in order to achieve an equitable outcome (*Libya v Malta* 1985: 47; the *Jan Mayen* case 1993: 61–2; Churchill and Lowe 1999: 187; *Cameroon v Nigeria* 2002: 441–2). On the other hand, the court could decide that the equidistance method should not be used, owing to special circumstances, and could apply another method entirely (that is, rather than drawing then adjusting an equidistance line). For example, in *Nicaragua v Honduras* (2007: 90), the Court held that there were special circumstances, such as the geographical configuration of the coast, which precluded the application of the equidistance principle. Here, the Court further noted that there might be factors that make application of the equidistance method inappropriate, but that the method remains the general rule (*Nicaragua v Honduras* 2007: 86, 90). In all three situations (that is, customary law, the 1958 Continental Shelf Convention and UNCLOS), the ultimate aim is reaching an equitable outcome.

The ICJ, in *Libya v Malta* (1985: 39–40), identified some of the equitable principles applicable to maritime delimitation cases. These include: the principle that there is to be no question of refashioning geography or compensating for the inequalities of nature; the principle of non-encroachment by one party on the natural prolongation of the other, that is, that the coastal State enjoys sovereign rights over the continental shelf off its coasts to the full extent authorised by international law in the relevant circumstances; the principle of respect due to all such relevant circumstances; the principle that, although all States are equal before the law and are entitled to equal treatment, equity does not necessarily imply equality, nor does it seek to make equal what nature has made unequal; and the principle that there can be no question of distributive justice. Just as with the delimitation of the territorial sea, for the continental shelf, the circumstances that the Court has found relevant to the delimitation of the continental shelf include proportionality, coastal configurations and the presence of islands (*North Sea Continental Shelf* cases 1969: 54; *Libya v Malta* 1985: 57; *Tunisia v Libya* 1982: 88; Freestone *et al.* 2006: 150–9; Dundua 2006–7: 53–68). These mainly relate to geographic features and can therefore not be applied to the CDM. In addition, the courts have been clear in stating that economic factors, particularly the relative wealth of the countries involved, are not relevant considerations in the process of delimitation and do not constitute special circumstances (*Tunisia v Libya* 1982: 77; *Libya v Malta* 1985: 41; *Gulf of Maine* case 1984; Guinea/Guinea Bissau arbitration 1986; Ahnish 1994: 90–2).

The rule for delimitation of the *EEZ and/or fishing zone* is practically identical to that regarding the delimitation of the continental shelf. In the *Gulf of Maine* case (1984: 299–300), which concerned both the continental shelf and EEZ, the ICJ specified that general international law in every maritime delimitation requires that delimitation: must be effected by agreement between the concerned States or (where agreement cannot be reached) by recourse to a third party, and must be based on the application of equitable criteria and the use of practical methods to achieve an equitable result. The Court stated that this rule represents the fundamental norm of customary international law governing maritime delimitation. Likewise, the provision of UNCLOS regarding delimitation of the EEZ is identical to that regarding the continental shelf. According to UNCLOS (Article 74.1), the delimitation of the EEZ should be effected by agreement on the basis of international law, to reach an equitable solution. In most cases regarding delimitation of the EEZ, the ICJ has been asked to delimit a single maritime boundary for both the EEZ and the continental shelf, rather than just for the EEZ alone. Instances include *Nicaragua v Honduras*, *Cameroon v Nigeria*, the *Gulf of Maine* case, the Guinea/Guinea Bissau arbitration and the Canada/France arbitration In these cases, the Court has also followed its decision in the *Gulf of Maine* case. For example, in the Guinea/Guinea Bissau arbitration (1986: 289), the Tribunal stated that the objective of finding an equitable solution is a rule of international law, and that the application of this rule requires the consideration of factors and the application of methods, which the Tribunal can select.

Applying these equitable rules to the CDM, achieving an equitable outcome would require consideration of relevant factors, although the exact factors to be considered will differ from those relevant to maritime border delimitation cases. In maritime border delimitation, relevant factors include the presence of islands and the configuration of coasts, which have no direct relevance to the issue of equitable distribution of CDM projects, because they relate mainly to the physical and/or geographic characteristics of maritime zones. The ICJ has also pointed out that the aim of delimitation is not to change geography or refashion nature, and that delimitation therefore does not aim at addressing natural inequalities (*North Sea Continental Shelf* cases 1969: 49–50; *Libya v Malta* 1985: 39–40; Oude Elferink 1994: 51; Ahnish 1994: 86–7).

Likewise in the case of the CDM, the goal of equity should not be that all countries should host the same number of projects, irrespective of the reality of their circumstances and limitations in this regard (such as limited emission reduction potential), as this would likely result in limiting the number of projects that can be hosted by the latter group of countries. This is discussed in greater detail in Chapter 5. As noted by the ICJ in the *North Sea Continental Shelf* cases, delimitation is not a question of 'rendering the situation of a State with an extensive coastline similar to that of a State with a restricted coastline'. Extending this to the CDM suggests that equitable distribution of CDM projects does not necessarily mean equal distribution – relevant factors should be taken into consideration when ascertaining how projects should be distributed.

4.2 Deep seabed regime

The deep seabed regime is governed by UNCLOS and the 1994 Implementing Agreement.[2] According to UNCLOS, the seabed, ocean floor and subsoil beyond the limits of national jurisdiction, collectively referred to as 'the Area', together with the resources found in them, are the common heritage of mankind (UNCLOS, Article 136). The legal status of the Area is outlined in Article 137, which prohibits countries from exercising sovereignty over the Area or its resources, and provides that the resources of the Area are vested in mankind as a whole.

It is important to note that exploitation of deep seabed resources is yet to commence. As such, there are no practical examples of the regime's application of distributive justice, whether through the common heritage

---

2 The changes made to Part XI by the Implementing Agreement relate to issues such as production limitations, mandatory technology transfer and the decision-making power of the International Seabed Authority. The common heritage concept as applied under UNCLOS, including the equitable sharing requirement, remained unchanged by the Agreement.

concept or otherwise. Nonetheless, the regime does provide some guidance on how resources should be distributed, and these are examined briefly below to see how they relate to the CDM.

The sharing provisions of the deep seabed regime are found mainly in Article 140 of UNCLOS, which provides that activities in the Area should be carried out for the benefit of mankind as a whole, taking account of the interests and needs of developing countries and peoples who have not gained self-governing status. It further requires the International Seabed Authority to provide for the equitable sharing of financial and other economic benefits derived from activities in the Area, in accordance with Article 160.2(f)(i) of UNCLOS.

This article requires the Authority, through its Assembly, to establish the rules, regulations and procedures for equitable sharing, again taking into particular consideration the interests and needs of developing countries and peoples who have not attained full independence or other self-governing status. However, the Authority has not yet established these distributional rules, and it is not clear when exactly these rules will be established.[3] It can, however, be expected that the rules will be established in accordance with the principles of the regime, such as the common heritage of mankind concept and the consideration of the needs of certain countries.

The concept of the common heritage of mankind was proposed by Maltese Ambassador Arvid Pardo, requesting that the use of the seabed and the ocean floor be undertaken for the benefit of mankind as a whole, and that the net financial benefits derived be used primarily to promote the development of poor countries (UNGA 1967). The concept advocates that the benefits derived from the 'common heritage' should not just be shared by a few members/ countries, but should profit all of mankind, and the benefits derived from the use of these resources should be shared internationally (Joyner 1998: 223).

The common heritage concept has been the subject of a lot of discussion and debate in international law. There is, as yet, no generally accepted definition of the concept and no general view regarding its status in international law (Errin 1984: 404; Frakes 2003: 409–410; Egede 2011: 66–73). However, as provided under the deep seabed regime, the concept has four elements: non-appropriation, equitable sharing of benefits, international management and exclusive peaceful use (UNCLOS, Articles 137.1, 137.2, 140.2 and 141). As the focus of this book is distributive justice, the element that is relevant to our discussion is the element of equitable sharing of benefits.

---

3   The International Seabed Authority is still in the process of establishing the various rules, regulations and procedures required by UNCLOS. It has, for example, issued the regulations on prospecting and exploration for polymetallic nodules and polymetallic sulphides in the Area. See 'Mining Code'. Online. Available at: www.isa.org.jm/en/mcode (accessed 3 May 2013).

Unfortunately, this element is not defined in UNCLOS and has not been defined by the regime, and, as the Authority has not yet defined the rules for distribution of resources, it is unknown how the concept will be applied under the regime. There are no examples that can be relied on to use to infer lessons for the CDM. The only guidance that UNCLOS provides on this matter is: it requires particular consideration of the interests and needs of developing States and peoples who have not attained full independence or other self-governing status (UNCLOS, Article 160.2(f)(i)).

In conclusion, although the deep seabed regime has not established the precise rules for distribution, nor has it defined its use of the common heritage of mankind concept, it does require that the interests and needs of specific groups of countries (in this case, developing countries) should be considered in order to achieve equitable sharing.

4.3 Fisheries regime

The international law of fisheries can be found in UNCLOS and addresses various issues relating to fisheries, particularly their conservation and management (UNCLOS, Articles 61–3). UNCLOS provides that coastal States have sovereign rights for the purpose of exploring, exploiting, conserving and managing the living and non-living natural resources in their EEZ, which includes fish stocks (UNCLOS, Article 56.1). This section focuses on the aspect of the fisheries regime that deals with access to resources.

In this regard, one important characteristic of fish is their migratory nature. Many fish stocks migrate between the EEZs of several countries and/or between EEZs and the high seas. The fish stocks that straddle the EEZs of two or more countries, or that cross the EEZ boundary of one country into the EEZ of another or several countries, are usually referred to as shared, joint or transboundary stocks (hereinafter referred to as transboundary stocks). Fish stocks that straddle or move across a country's EEZ boundary and the adjacent high seas, or that are to be found both within a country's EEZ and the adjacent high seas, are called straddling stocks (UNCLOS, Article 63). Although 'highly migratory' fish stocks are not defined in UNCLOS, it does contain an agreed list of species considered highly migratory (UNCLOS, Annex I). These generally have a wide geographic distribution both within and outside countries' EEZs and migrate through high seas and countries' EEZs during their life cycle (Christopherson 1996: 363).

This section focuses on these transboundary, straddling and highly migratory fish stocks and, in particular, how access to them is allocated or determined. An examination of the fisheries regime and its provisions relating to these fish stocks shows that the regime does not contain rules or guidance on how access to them should be determined. Instead, UNCLOS only contains rules relating to their conservation and development.

Regarding transboundary fish stocks, Article 63.1 requires countries to agree on measures necessary for their conservation and development, but does not provide specific guidance on what the necessary measures could be. Although there are bilateral and regional agreements regulating transboundary stocks, again, most of these relate to their conservation and management, rather than access to them. For straddling fish stocks, two sets of rules apply. The rule regarding fishing in the EEZ is that the coastal country has sovereign rights to explore, exploit, conserve and manage the natural resources, including fisheries, in its EEZ (UNCLOS, Article 56). Fishing in the high seas is governed by the 'freedom of the high seas' rule, which means that all countries have the right to fish in the high seas, subject to obligations to conserve and cooperate (UNCLOS Articles 63.2, 87, 116–20). The 1995 Fish Stocks Agreement provides additional guidance on issues relating to the conservation and management of straddling and highly migratory fish stocks, through provisions requiring, among other things, information sharing, biodiversity protection, and pollution and waste minimisation (Fish Stocks Agreement, Articles 2 and 5). Other than the fact that these provisions are mainly procedural and not substantive, they also relate to conservation and management and are not, therefore, relevant for distributive justice.

The rules with regard to highly migratory stocks are similar to those for straddling stocks. UNCLOS requires fishing nations to cooperate directly or through appropriate international organisations to ensure conservation and promote optimum utilisation of highly migratory stocks. It provides further that, in regions where there are no appropriate international organisations, fishing nations should cooperate to establish such an organisation and participate in its work (UNCLOS, Article 64). These provisions are very succinct and are expanded on in the Fish Stocks Agreement. The objective and principles of the Agreement relating to highly migratory stocks are identical to those relating to straddling stocks: they are primarily concerned with the conservation and management of these species, rather than with access to them (Fish Stocks Agreement, Articles 2, 5 and 8).

Consequently, the provisions of the fisheries regime will not be examined in more detail, as they are not directly relevant to the issue of the distribution of CDM projects.

4.4 International watercourses regime

This section examines the international legal rules governing the use of shared watercourses, that is, freshwater resources that are shared by more than one country or parts of which are found in more than one country. With regard to the use of, or access to, shared watercourses, one of the basic rules is the requirement for equitable and reasonable sharing of the watercourses (Amr 2002: 112–113; Shelton 2007: 647–648; Birnie *et al.* 2009: 541).

As far back as 1966, the (non-binding) Helsinki Rules provided that basin States are entitled to a reasonable and equitable share in the beneficial uses of the waters of an international drainage basin (Helsinki Rules, Article IV). In the *Gabcikovo-Nagymaros Project* case, the ICJ referred to Hungary's right to an equitable and reasonable sharing of the resources of the shared watercourse (*Gabcikovo-Nagymaros Project* case, 54). In his separate opinion in the *Kasikili/Sedudu Island* case, Judge Kooijmans, although falling short of declaring that this was a rule of customary international law, noted that the rule has been widely accepted both for the navigational and the non-navigational uses of international watercourses (*Kasikili/Sedudu Island* case, 1150–2).

Relevant treaty law on international watercourses is the Convention on the Law of the Non-navigational Uses of International Watercourses. According to the Convention, watercourse States are to use international watercourses in an equitable and reasonable manner (International Watercourses Convention, Article 5.1). This Convention is, however, not yet in force, as it has not yet acquired the requisition number of ratifications. Nevertheless, as noted above, the principle of equitable and reasonable utilisation is the most widely endorsed principle relating to the use of shared watercourses and is regarded by some as the fundamental norm governing this area of law (McCaffrey 2003: 325; Sands 2003: 462; Birnie *et al.* 2009: 541–2). Consequently, this principle of equitable and reasonable utilisation probably reflects customary international law regarding allocation of, or access to, shared watercourses, and this section focuses on this principle.

The Convention requires watercourse States to use international watercourses in an equitable and reasonable manner. This, inter alia, means that these countries should use and develop international watercourses with the aim of ensuring their optimal and sustainable use. In doing this, the watercourse States should take account of the interests of all watercourse States concerned and the need for adequate protection of the watercourse (Watercourses Convention, Article 5.1). The Convention further requires watercourse States to participate in the use, development and protection of international watercourses in an equitable and reasonable manner, with such participation including both the right to utilise watercourses and the duty to cooperate in their protection and development (Watercourses Convention, Article 5.2).

The Convention does not expressly define 'equitable and reasonable' use. Instead, it provides guidance as to what can be deemed equitable and reasonable, by outlining some of the factors for determining whether a use is equitable and reasonable. It then identifies some of these factors and circumstances, including: geographic and other factors of a natural character; the social and economic needs of the watercourse States concerned; the population dependent on the watercourse in each watercourse State; the effects of the use or uses of the watercourses in one watercourse State on other watercourse States; existing and potential uses of the watercourse;

conservation, protection, development and economy of use of the water resources of the watercourse and the costs of measures taken to that effect; and the availability of alternatives, of comparable value, to a particular planned or existing use (Watercourses Convention, Article 6.1). Grzybowski *et al.* divides these factors into two categories: natural factors (such as climatic and geographic factors) and human-related factors (such as the social and economic needs of watercourse States and the existing and potential uses of the watercourses) (Grzybowski *et al.* 2010: 142).

The starting point for the use of shared watercourses is the equality of States and their equality of right to use shared watercourses (Amr 2002: 135; McCaffrey 2003: 328). The ICJ, in the *Gabcikovo-Nagymaros Project* case, refers to the 'perfect equality of all riparian States' as an essential feature of the use of the shared watercourse (*Gabcikovo-Nagymaros Project* case, 54). This equality of right does not mean an equal division of the shared waters, but that all the parties have an equal right to use the shared waters, owing to the equality of independent States (McCaffrey 2003: 330; Birnie *et al.* 2009: 542). Likewise with the CDM, all countries have an equal right to participate in the CDM, but this does not necessarily mean there should be an equal distribution of CDM projects.

Applying the principle of equitable utilisation as conceived in the international watercourses regime to the CDM, this means that, to ensure an equitable geographic distribution of CDM projects, all relevant factors should be taken into account. These factors will, in most cases, be specific to the issue being considered. For example, in the case of shared watercourses, the Convention identifies the population dependent on the watercourses, the existing and potential uses of the watercourses, and the social and economic needs of the watercourse States concerned as factors to be considered in determining equitable and reasonable use (Watercourses Convention, Article 6). The climate change regime takes this same approach, requiring consideration of countries' responsibility, capability and needs.

In conclusion, as applied under the international watercourses regime, equitable utilisation requires consideration of a set of factors directly relevant to the regime, in order to achieve an equitable outcome.

4.5 Conclusion

The above regimes, particularly the international watercourses regime and maritime boundary delimitation, show that an equitable outcome very much depends on the specific law, issue or circumstance under consideration. None of the regimes defines what an equitable outcome is. Rather, they identify some of the factors that should be taken into consideration in order to achieve such an outcome (with the exception of the fisheries regime, which does not contain any relevant rules).

Consequently, the conclusion from the above analysis is that distributive justice in international law takes a 'process-based' approach, being the outcome of a process in which certain factors are taken into consideration. In the case of international watercourses, for example, an equitable outcome is achieved when factors such as the needs and uses of States, as well as the geographic and hydrographic factors of the watercourses, are taken into consideration.

These factors are specific to the particular regime being considered and should not be generalised. When these factors are fully accounted for, the outcome of this process would be considered just or equitable. There is, therefore, no 'one-size-fits-all' outcome.

5 Meaning of equitable geographic distribution of CDM projects

This chapter draws together the discussion in Chapters 3 and 4, both of which considered what equity and distributive justice under the CDM should look like, using an analysis of how equity and distributive justice are achieved under international law. These chapters concluded that, in international law, distributive justice is usually achieved through a process that takes certain specified factors into consideration, with the resulting outcome considered equitable or just. This reflects the approach to equity taken in the climate change regime, and it can therefore be expected that it should be the approach to equitable distribution under the CDM. Following on from this conclusion, this chapter focuses on the actual meaning of equitable geographic distribution of CDM projects.

First, applying the above conclusion to the CDM, it means that equitable distribution should be regarded as the result of a process that takes certain factors into consideration, rather than as a set or predetermined outcome. As highlighted, these factors are not generic, but, instead, tend to be specific to the particular regime being considered. Further to this, this chapter identifies the factors that should be considered in order to achieve an equitable distribution of projects under the CDM. Upon identifying these factors, this chapter then provides a working definition of equitable geographic distribution of CDM projects based on the discussions in this and previous chapters.

5.1 Possible elements of equitable geographic distribution

The discussions in Chapters 3 and 4 show that regimes consider specific factors in their efforts to achieve an equitable outcome, and these factors are not universal – they vary from regime to regime. An examination of the CDM identifies seven possible factors for achieving an equitable outcome: equality, emission reduction potential, need/sustainable development potential, responsibility, capability, population and preferential treatment. However, a closer look at these factors in the context of the operation and objectives of the CDM shows that the only two factors that should be specifically considered for determining an equitable outcome under the CDM are emission reduction potential and need/sustainable development potential. Nonetheless, this section examines all the possible elements below and explains why these are the only two that should be specifically considered.

5.1.1 Equality

Equitable distribution of CDM projects does not mean equal distribution of CDM projects. Strict equality in the distribution of CDM projects would mean that all countries should receive the same number of projects or generate the same amount of CERs, irrespective of their circumstances or differences between them.

For example, as at March 2013, there were 6,556 registered CDM projects, which were expected to generate about 848 million CERs annually (CDM Pipeline, 1 March 2013), and there were 129 eligible developing countries. Equality would require that each developing country should host about fifty-one projects each, or produce about 6.5 million CERs annually (6,556 and 848 million divided by 129). This seems like an attractive outcome, particularly considering the current distribution, where one country (China) hosts over 3,000 projects, some countries host several hundred, and many countries host none at all. Nevertheless, there is a problem with this solution, which is that strict equality does not allow consideration of relevant differences among countries.

In the case of the CDM, a key relevant difference is countries' differing CDM hosting potential, due to their different GHG emission levels. Not all countries can host fifty-one CDM projects or generate 6.5 million CERs annually. For example, countries' 2005 emissions data showed that about thirty countries produced fewer than 6.5 million tonnes of CO_2e emissions annually (Climate Analysis Indicators Tool (CAIT), 2005 data).[1] It is, therefore, impossible for them to reduce their emissions by 6.6 million, when they produce less than this amount, even assuming that all of a country's GHG emissions can be optimally reduced through the CDM. Limiting the number of projects countries would be allowed to host to the number that the countries with the lowest GHG emission reduction potential can host would ensure equality. This would, however, obviously be counter-productive and contrary to the objectives of the CDM.

Equity does not require that countries with limited potential to host CDM projects should be expected to host the same number of projects as those that have greater potential. For this reason, strict equality is not suitable for achieving equity under the CDM, as it would lead to a perverse outcome, which would neither benefit countries nor contribute to the objectives of the CDM.

---

1   The reasons for the use of the 2005 data are explained in Chapter 6 – these are the most comprehensive data (that is, covering the greatest number of GHGs).

5.1.2 Emission reduction potential

To ensure that the CDM achieves its objective of reducing GHG emissions, countries' emission reduction potential, determined by their GHG emission levels, must be taken into consideration. As noted above, equitable geographic distribution cannot mean equal distribution of projects or CERs, because countries have varying levels of GHG emissions and, hence, varying levels of emission reduction potential. Uruguay, which produces about 42 million tonnes of CO_2e emissions annually, cannot be expected to host the same number of projects as Indonesia, which produces in excess of 2 billion tonnes of CO_2e emissions annually (CAIT, 2005 data).

Countries' emissions data are available from the World Resources Institute's CAIT. This tool contains the GHG emissions of most countries and can help with calculating a country's potential for GHG emission reductions. Data from the CAIT show that all eligible developing countries have the potential to reduce their GHG emissions. Chapter 6 discusses this issue further and classifies countries according to their GHG emission reduction potential.

It is important to note here that these figures only take into consideration countries' actual emissions. The question is whether this is fair to those developing countries that have lower than expected emissions owing to, inter alia, lack of access to energy. Globally, nearly 1.3 billion people lack access to electricity (IEA 2012). Sub-Saharan African countries are the worst off in this regard, having the largest concentrations of people without access to modern energy sources (IEA 2012; Hailun 2012). What this translates to in practical terms is that, for many of these countries, they have such low GHG emissions simply because they are poor and lack basic goods that, although GHG-emitting, would improve their standard of living. The question, then, is whether their current levels of energy consumption should be maintained because of the struggle to combat climate change. Or is there room for their energy consumption to increase, despite this struggle?

In the IEA's new policies scenario, global energy demand is expected to grow by more than one-third up to 2035 (IEA 2012). In 2010, UN Secretary-General Ban Ki-moon launched the Sustainable Energy for All initiative, which has, as one of its objectives, ensuring universal access to modern energy. The UNFCCC recognises that developing countries need access to resources required to achieve sustainable social and economic development and that, in order for them to progress towards this goal, their energy consumption will need to grow (UNFCCC, Preamble, paragraph 22). It is, therefore, clear that, for many developing countries, their energy consumption will and should increase, as will their GHG emissions.

This is where the issue of 'suppressed demand' comes in. Suppressed demand refers to a situation where the consumption of energy services is low, not because of a lack of demand, but because the demand is not being met. The reasons for the demand for energy services not being met, or being 'suppressed', could be because households cannot afford the cost of energy, or because the available energy services are insufficient to meet demand. The suppressed demand approach recognises that, as incomes increase, energy costs reduce and access to energy increases, energy consumption will also increase, and GHG emissions patterns will therefore change (Gwage 2012).

The CDM allows for a suppressed demand scenario to be addressed when establishing a baseline. As explained in Chapter 2, the project baseline for a CDM project is, simply put, a 'pre-project' scenario, representing the level of GHG emissions produced in the absence of the CDM project. CDM projects are then credited for reducing emissions below this baseline (one CER per tonne of emission reduction achieved). The suppressed demand approach under the CDM allows for a situation where the 'pre-project' emissions are low because basic human needs are not being met, and it would be difficult, if not impossible (and undesirable), to further reduce emissions below this level.

The CDM guidelines define a suppressed demand situation as one where 'a minimum service level to meet basic human needs, as defined above, was unavailable to the end user of the service prior to the implementation of the project activity'.[2] The guidelines set out how to address this situation to identify both the baseline technology/measure (for example, in the case of lighting, would the relevant households have been using small wick lamps or incandescent lamps if they could afford them) and the baseline service level (what level of consumption would have occurred in the baseline scenario if the households could afford the energy service). The result could be that, for example, although household A does not have access to any electricity because of suppressed demand, it would have been using a small wick lamp for 6 hours a day, if it could afford to do so. This would then be taken as the baseline and used to calculate the baseline level of GHG emissions (the emissions that would be produced by burning a wick lamp for 6 hours a day), and reductions below this baseline by the project would then be credited to the project. This is a very simplified description, but gives a general idea of the process.

It is, therefore, important, when considering countries' emission reduction potential, to consider not just their current emissions levels, but to account for suppressed demand. However, what is apparent from the definition of suppressed demand is that it is a consequence of countries' lack of sustainable development – it arises where countries lack the minimum service level to meet basic human needs. Therefore, as a country develops and its need level reduces, suppressed demand would also reduce, as, for instance, access to energy improves. Consequently, rather than considering

---

2   'Guidelines on the Consideration of Suppressed Demand in CDM Methodologies.' Online. Available at: http://cdm.unfccc.int/Reference/Guidclarif/meth/meth_guid41.pdf (accessed 3 May 2013).

suppressed demand as a factor on its own, or considering it in addition to countries' emission reduction potential, suppressed demand should be accounted for through consideration of countries' sustainable development potential or need. Adequate consideration of this will automatically ensure consideration of suppressed demand. Sustainable development potential and need are discussed in greater detail in the next section.

5.1.3 Need/sustainable development potential

The reference to potential is often a reference to emission reduction potential. However, it is not enough to only consider countries' emission reduction potentials and their opportunities for cost-effective reductions, as these only measure the CDM's objective of promoting cost-effective emission reductions. As sustainable development is one of the objectives of the CDM, in order to achieve this objective, another kind of potential that should also be considered is the sustainable development potential of countries.

Sustainable development has been defined as 'development that meets the needs of the present without compromising the ability of future generations to meet their own needs'. Consideration of needs (particularly the essential needs of the world's poor) is considered a key concept of sustainable development (Brundtland Report: paragraph 1; Sands 2003: 252; Birnie *et al.* 2007: 53–4). This is recognised in many international treaties. Chapter 3 shows that the international climate change regime contains this requirement, and provides that countries' special interests and needs should be considered, and that they should be given preferential treatment in consideration of their needs. The discussion in Chapter 4 also shows that both the deep seabed and international watercourses regimes also require consideration of countries' needs in order to achieve an equitable outcome. Schachter (1991: 16) notes that, 'it is undeniable that the fulfilment of the needs of the poor and disadvantaged countries has been recognised as a normative principle which is central to the idea of equity and distributive justice.' As one of the objectives of the CDM is to promote sustainable development, then the consideration of countries' need is necessary for ensuring equity under the CDM.

For example, in relation to economic growth and poverty eradication, different countries are at differing stages of development, and their needs in this regard vary. Countries such as Timor-Leste, Chad and Afghanistan are classified as LDCs because they have low human development[3] levels

---

3 Human development is defined by UNDP as development that ensures peoples' well-being, empowerment and agency, and justice. It is measured using the indicators of life expectancy, adult literacy, gross enrolment in education, purchasing power parity and income. See UNDP, *Human Development Report 2010, The Real Wealth of Nations:*

and greater developmental needs, whereas countries such as Singapore, Barbados, Qatar and the Republic of Korea (which the Convention classifies as developing countries) are actually classified as having very high human development levels and, therefore, fewer developmental needs (United Nations Development Programme (UNDP) Human Development Index (HDI) 2012). This is because the latter countries have relatively high life expectancy, high adult literacy and gross enrolment in education, as well as a decent standard of living measured by their gross domestic product.[4] Consequently, such countries have, for example, fewer economic, developmental and capacity needs than the LDCs. Consideration of countries' levels of need should form part of efforts to achieve equitable geographic distribution of CDM projects.

In this book, the factor of 'need' is, therefore, used to indicate countries' sustainable development needs or potential. There is, however, the question of how to measure a country's level of need. The UNFCCC and Kyoto Protocol, although not explicitly defining need, identify categories of countries whose needs and interests should be taken into particular consideration, including: SIDS, countries with low-lying coastal areas, and land-locked and transit countries (UNFCCC, Preamble, paragraph 19, and Articles 4.8 and 4.9). More specifically, the CDM identifies three groups of countries as requiring particular consideration: SIDS, LDCs and African countries (Decision 1/CMP.2, paragraphs 39 and 41; Decision 2/CMP.3, paragraph 34; and Decision 2/CMP.4, paragraphs 53, 55 and 56).

Regarding what constitutes the special need of LDCs, SIDS and African countries, the most obvious is the need for sustainable development. This is particularly so in the case of LDCs, which are the countries with the lowest human development and are, therefore, the most in need of sustainable development. Most African countries and SIDS are among the countries with the lowest human development. For example, thirty-three of the fifty-three countries in the African region are on the UN LDCs list; that is thirty-three out of a total of forty-nine LDCs. Likewise, twelve of the thirty-eight SIDS are also LDCs. However, several SIDS are actually among the countries with the highest human development, such as Singapore and Barbados (UNDP HDI 2012). Classifying countries broadly by these groups, therefore, does not accurately differentiate among countries according to their need, as, within these groups, countries' sustainable development potentials and needs vary widely.

Pathways to Human Development (New York: UNDP, 2010), 13 and 22. It is, therefore, about more than peoples' or countries' incomes.

4   These are the indicators used by UNDP to measure countries' human development levels. See http://hdr.undp.org/en/humandev/ 'The Human Development concept' (UNDP, 16 February 2011). See 'Human development index 2011 and its components' http://hdr.undp.org/en/media/HDR_2011_EN_Table1.pdf (accessed 8 March 2013).

This book uses the HDI as a more accurate measurement of countries' sustainable development potential or need. The HDI measures human development in three basic dimensions: health (calculated using life expectancy at birth), educational attainment (calculated using mean and expected years of schooling) and standard of living (calculated using gross national income per capita). The basic use of HDI is to rank countries by level of 'human development'.[5] The HDI has not been generally accepted as a measure of human development and has been criticised for, inter alia, not including environmental indicators in its assessment (McGillivray 1993; Sagara and Najam 1998). Nonetheless, it is a widely used measure of human development and is regarded as a more complete assessment of a country's development than GDP or GNP, because, unlike these two indicators, it assesses, not only economic, but also social, development (Globerman and Shapiro 2002; Dias *et al.* 2006).

5.1.4 Capability

Capability or ability to address a problem is relevant to the distribution of CDM projects, particularly when capability is taken to include technical capacity to host CDM projects, for instance, in terms of project development and implementation experience. Such capability or ability should be a relevant factor in the distribution of projects, not in the sense of giving preference to countries that have greater capabilities, but, rather, the opposite. One of the sustainable development benefits of the CDM is increased capacity, including capacity to develop and implement sustainable and environmentally friendly projects and activities. Ability, or rather lack of it, should be regarded as a measure of sustainable development in developing countries.

Hence, countries with less capacity should be regarded as having greater sustainable development potential in this regard, just as countries with greater needs are regarded as having greater sustainable development potential. Enabling them to host projects and providing them with the associated increased capacity should be regarded as contributing to the sustainable development objective of the CDM. If countries with greater capacity were given preference on the basis of this capacity, and lack of capacity counted against countries, this would amount to 'putting the cart before the horse' – expecting countries to already have the benefit (capability or capacity) that the CDM is meant to provide them with.

For example, one of the needs of developing countries identified by the climate change regime is their need for capacity building (UNFCCC, Articles 5(b) and (c), 7 and 9.2(d); and Kyoto Protocol, Article 10(e)). However,

5   See 'Human Development Index'. Online. Available at: http://hdr.undp.org/en/statistics/hdi/ (accessed 2 March 2013).

rather than being a separate element, it is, in the context of the CDM, a measure of countries' need and sustainable development.

5.1.5 Population

One important consideration in the distribution of CDM projects is countries' population. It cannot really be expected that a country with a very small population should host the same number of projects as a country with a very large population. This is mainly owing to the fact that a country with a larger population will almost invariably have more GHG emissions and also need more resources to sustain its population. This could be taken to suggest that countries such as China, India and Indonesia should, simply because of their larger populations, host more projects than countries such as Panama, Jamaica and Lesotho, which have much smaller populations in comparison.

However, population should not be a separate consideration for equitable distribution of projects. It is not independently linked to either of the CDM's objectives (of reducing GHG emissions and promoting sustainable development), nor is it directly relevant to achievement of these objectives. Whereas emission reduction potential and need are directly linked to, and relevant for, the CDM's objectives of reducing GHG emission and promoting sustainable development, population does not have any such direct link, except to the extent already covered by the factors of emission reduction potential and need.

First, population is, to a very great extent, already factored into countries' GHG emission levels and emission reduction potentials. One of the drivers of emissions in countries is the size of their population and population growth (Metz *et al.* 2007: 178–9; OECD/IEA 2007: 180, 401). This is partly because the larger the size of the population, the more energy is consumed, and efforts to meet the increasing energy needs of a growing population have a direct impact on the climate (IEA 2012), as more than 60 per cent of GHG emissions come from energy production and consumption (OECD/IEA 2007: 3). For example, a country such as China is the world's largest GHG emitter, partly because it has the world's largest population, although there are other factors involved, such as rapid industrialisation and the nature of energy consumed (OECD/IEA 2007: 82).

For example, China's per capita emissions are low (5.5 tonnes per person) compared with other developing countries such as Qatar (68.9 tonnes per person – the highest in the world) and Equatorial Guinea (18 tonnes per person). However, looking at total emissions, China's are the highest globally (7.2 billion tonnes), whereas Qatar's are 61 million tonnes, and Equatorial Guinea's are 11 million tonnes. These figures are obviously a function of these countries' populations – 1.3 billion in China, over 2 million in Qatar and about 0.7 million in Equatorial Guinea. A country such as China can therefore be expected to host more projects than a country such as Equatorial Guinea, not simply because of its larger population, as this will not directly contribute to achievement of either of the CDM's objectives, but because it has a larger emission reduction potential and can therefore contribute to the CDM's objective of reducing GHG emissions.

With relation to need and the CDM's objective of promoting sustainable development, population again is not a directly relevant factor. For example, although Brazil has the fifth largest population in the world (fourth largest in the developing world), it only has medium need, because of its high human development (UNDP HDI 2012). Its large population should not, therefore, be a basis for it to be expected to host more projects than Pakistan, which has the next highest population, but has very high need because of its low human development. In this context, population is irrelevant, as the relevant consideration is countries' sustainable development potential and how much the CDM can contribute to this. Adding the population element would simply distort the picture of how CDM projects should be distributed among developing countries.

In addition, presumably, as a country hosts more CDM projects, its sustainable development levels will improve, and its need will reduce. For example, assume that 10 CDM projects would contribute as much to Equatorial Guinea's sustainable development as 100 CDM projects would to China's (because of the difference in the size of their populations). If Equatorial Guinea and China were each to host ten CDM projects, then Equatorial Guinea's need would reduce significantly, because of the contribution of these projects to its sustainable development, whereas China's would not reduce at the same rate (because it requires more projects to achieve a comparable level of sustainable development). Under the CDM, China would then be expected to continue to receive more projects, while Equatorial Guinea would not (or would not be expected to receive as many). This adequately takes account of these countries' populations, and there is, therefore, no benefit to taking each country's population into account, independently of their need.

Consequently, population is not a factor that should be given specific consideration in efforts to achieve equitable geographic distribution. Although it is an important factor, it is already implicitly covered by the factors of emission reduction potential and need, and a separate, independent consideration of population will not contribute to achieving equity under the CDM.

5.1.6 Preferential treatment

Most international regimes and agreements, in their efforts to achieve an equitable outcome, provide developing countries with some form of preferential treatment, in recognition of their greater need or lower capacity. Examples include the Stockholm Declaration, the Montreal Protocol and the UNFCCC. Such preferential treatment, rather than determining whether an outcome is equitable, is used to help achieve an equitable outcome. The Montreal Protocol, the UNFCCC, the International Tropical Timber Agreement and the World Trade Organization's generalised system of preferences all contain examples of such preferential treatment, based primarily on the principles of equity and common but differentiated responsibilities.

Equity sometimes requires positive discrimination. This is not unusual, especially in dealings between developed and developing countries, where developing countries often receive some form of preferential treatment, usually in consideration of their special needs, interests and circumstances. Cullet notes that 'differential treatment is intrinsically linked to the notion of equity' (Cullet 2003: 29). According to Rajamani, real differences exist between states, and 'norms of differential treatment recognize and respond to these real differences between states by instituting different standards for different states or groups of states' (Rajamani 2006: 1).

For example, the Montreal Protocol allows developing countries to delay by 10 years their compliance with the control measures contained in the Protocol (Montreal Protocol, Article 5). Under the UNFCCC, developing countries are generally given far fewer obligations than developed countries, and, under the Kyoto Protocol, they do not have any mitigation targets, whereas developed countries do (UNFCCC, Articles 3 and 4; Kyoto Protocol, Article 10). The CDM, too, is an instrument of differentiation between developed and developing countries. It gives developing countries the opportunity to participate in climate change mitigation without taking on the kind of binding emission reduction commitments developed countries have, and also offers them the sustainable development benefits that CDM projects are supposed to provide. Accordingly, there is support for giving preferential treatment on the basis of need, in order to achieve equity.

In the context of the CDM, it follows that preferential treatment should be given to the countries with the greatest need or lowest level of development, such as those countries with the lowest HDI. And there is already some preferential treatment given under the CDM. For example, LDCs are exempt from payment of the share-of-proceeds levy under the CDM, as well as the CDM registration fee. This is discussed further in Chapter 9. It is also important to determine what kind of preferential treatment countries should receive. The aim of preferential treatment under the CDM would be to improve countries' access to the mechanism and overcome the barriers to CDM hosting, thereby ensuring a more equitable distribution of projects among countries. Importantly also, it should be genuine preferential treatment, aimed at reducing, not increasing, dependency (that is, it should not amount to 'hand-outs'). The various forms of preferential treatment currently provided under the CDM regime are discussed in more detail in Chapter 9, which examines the regime's measures to promote equitable distribution.

5.2 Definition of equitable geographic distribution

The above analysis shows that the two factors that should be taken into consideration in order to achieve an equitable outcome under the CDM are countries' GHG emission reduction potential and their need (sustainable development potential). In addition, just as is seen in most international regimes, efforts to promote equitable geographic distribution should then be supported by preferential treatment, specifically in consideration of countries' need. All these should be taken into consideration and balanced in order to achieve a more equitable geographic distribution of CDM projects.

As Chapters 3 and 4 showed, in general, distributive justice in international law does not have a set definition or outcome. Instead, most regimes provide that certain factors should be considered in order to achieve an equitable outcome. Likewise, under the CDM, there can be no set outcome in terms of prescribing exactly how many projects or exactly what percentage of projects each developing country should host. Rather, equitable distribution of CDM projects would be the result of a process that gives all developing countries an equal right to participate in the CDM regime and to benefit from the sustainable development benefits of the CDM. This equal right does not mean an equal number of projects. Instead, it means a share of projects proportionate to each country's GHG emission reduction potential and need (sustainable development potential). These two factors represent the two objectives of the CDM and both need to be equally taken into consideration. In addition, efforts to achieve equitable distribution should also give preferential treatment, such as capacity building and financial support, to those countries with the greatest need, provided they also have emission reduction potential. This is in order to help these countries fulfil their CDM potential, which is calculated using their emission reduction and sustainable development potentials. Chapter 6 expands on countries' CDM potential.

In conclusion, an equitable geographic distribution of CDM projects is a distribution among countries based on their GHG emission reduction potential and their need or sustainable development potential. These factors make up countries' CDM potential, and they should determine the priority to be given to countries in terms of CDM hosting. A distribution that is the result of the consideration of these two factors can then be regarded as equitable. Paying serious, deliberate and explicit attention to equity in the distribution of projects will oblige investors to consider developing countries' need, together with their emission reduction potential, when selecting countries to invest in.

Furthermore, as noted in Chapter 2, countries are operating under a presumption that the distribution of CDM projects among countries is not equitable, and effort has been made to address this. The next chapter proves that this presumption is, in fact, correct. It shows how projects should be distributed among countries, using countries' emission reduction and sustainable development potentials as the measurements, and compares this with the current distribution to determine how the current distribution compares with this ideal distribution.

6 Distribution of CDM projects in practice

Is the current geographic distribution equitable?

Chapter 5 provided a definition for equitable geographic distribution of CDM projects and outlined the factors that need to be considered in order to achieve this outcome. Following on from this, this chapter focuses on the current distribution of CDM projects and considers whether it can be considered equitable using the definition of equitable distribution provided in Chapter 5.

This chapter contains a practical application of the conceptual discussions undertaken and conclusions reached in Chapters 3–5. Applying the factors of equitable geographic distribution identified in Chapter 5, this chapter determines whether the current geographic distribution of CDM projects is equitable or inequitable. As identified in Chapter 5, the factors of equitable distribution that determine countries' CDM potential are emission reduction potential and need. The current geographic distribution of projects is compared with this ideal distribution, with the aim of determining whether or not the current distribution fits this ideal.

The questions this chapter answers are 'what is the ideal distribution of CDM projects among countries?' and 'is the current distribution of CDM projects equitable?'

6.1 Need

As identified in Chapter 5, one of the factors that need to be considered when trying to achieve an equitable geographic distribution of projects is countries' sustainable development potential or need, and this section focuses on this factor.

Countries are classified according to their sustainable development potential using UNDP's human development as the measurement indicator. The latest HDI data available are for 2012, and it is these data that are used in this section (UNDP HDI 2012). Although it is possible to use the 2005 HDI data in order to be consistent with countries' GHG emissions data, the 2012 data are a more accurate measurement of countries' current development levels than the 2005 data. As the purpose of this section is not to compare countries' sustainable development potential with their GHG emission reduction potential, but to carry out a comparison among countries, it is better in this situation to be accurate. HDI data are available for all eligible developing countries,[1] with the exception of the Democratic People's Republic of Korea.

UNDP classifies countries into four groups based on quartiles of HDI distribution, as follows: very high, high, medium and low. This book adopts this classification, but modifies it slightly to fit the intention of the categorisation in this section, and also to match with the classification used in section 6.2. As such, countries are classified as follows: UNDP's low HDI = very high need; medium HDI = high need; high HDI = medium need; very high HDI = low need. Countries' actual HDI values are contained in Appendix B.

6.2 Emission reduction potential

All developing countries produce GHG emissions, and all therefore have the potential to reduce their GHG emissions. It is, however, unlikely that every country will be able to host as many projects as it has the potential to, largely owing to practical issues, specifically the size of the CDM market. As of March 2013, the CDM was expected to achieve annual reductions of approximately 848 million tonnes of CO_2e (CDM Pipeline, 1 March 2013). Annual developing country GHG emissions for 2005 are estimated to be about 25 billion tonnes of CO_2e (CAIT Version 7.0), which means that, annually, only about 3.4 per cent of developing countries' emissions are being reduced through the CDM.

This section classifies countries according to their GHG emission reduction potential, using their current emissions levels. The data used here are obtained from the World Resources Institute CAIT (CAIT Version 7.0). This database contains the total GHG emissions of all eligible developing countries, with the exception of Timor-Leste, Serbia and Montenegro. For Serbia and Montenegro, their 2005 GHG emission levels are computed together, and there are therefore no emissions data available for each country – only joint emissions data are available.[2] For Timor-Leste, this book uses data obtained from the United States Department of Energy's Carbon Dioxide Information Analysis Center, which was prepared for the UN. These data only consider CO_2 emissions from the burning of fossil fuels and cement manufacture, but not emissions from other gases, such as methane and

---

1 'Eligible developing countries' refers to those countries that are eligible to participate in the CDM, that is, those countries that currently meet the CDM requirements (Protocol ratification and DNA establishment). See Appendix A for a list of these countries. As of March 2013, there were 129 eligible developing countries.

2 This is because the data used are 2005 data, and, at this time, Serbia and Montenegro were a single country. The countries became independent of each other in 2006.

Table 6.1 Eligible developing countries and their sustainable development potential/ need

Low need (1)	Medium need (2)	High need (3)	Very high need (4)
Republic of Korea	Bahrain	Belize	Solomon Islands
Israel	Bahamas	Dominican Republic	São Tomé & Principe
Singapore	Uruguay	Fiji	Kenya
Qatar	Montenegro	Samoa	Bangladesh
Barbados	Kuwait	Jordan	Pakistan
Chile	Saudi Arabia	China	Angola
United Arab Emirates	Cuba	Turkmenistan	Myanmar
Argentina	Panama	Thailand	Cameroon
	Mexico	Maldives	Madagascar
	Costa Rica	Suriname	Tanzania
	Grenada	Gabon	Nigeria
	Libya	El Salvador	Senegal
	Malaysia	Bolivia	Mauritánia
	Serbia	Mongolia	Papua New Guinea
	Antigua & Barbuda	Paraguay	Nepal
	Trinidad & Tobago	Egypt	Lesotho
	Albania	Moldova	Togo
	Georgia	The Philippines	Yemen
	Lebanon	Uzbekistan	Haiti
	Iran	Syria	Uganda
	Peru	Guyana	Zambia
	Macedonia	Botswana	Djibouti
	Mauritius	Honduras	Gambia
	Bosnia & Herzegovina	Indonesia	Benin
	Azerbaijan	South Africa	Rwanda
	Oman	Kyrgyzstan	Côte D'Ivoire
	Brazil	Tajikistan	Comoros
	Jamaica	Vietnam	Malawi
	Armenia	Namibia	Sudan
	Saint Lucia	Nicaragua	Zimbabwe
	Ecuador	Morocco	Ethiopia
	Colombia	Iraq	Liberia
	Sri Lanka	Cape Verde	Guinea-Bissau
	Algeria	Guatemala	Sierra Leone
	Tunisia	Timor-Leste	Burundi
		Ghana	Guinea
		Equatorial Guinea	Eritrea
		India	Mali
		Cambodia	Burkina Faso
		Lao	Chad
		Bhutan	Mozambique
		Swaziland	Congo DR
			Niger

Source: UNDP HDI (2012).

nitrous oxide, nor does it consider emissions from land use, land-use change and forestry.[3]

The available data have some shortcomings, however. For all countries, their total CO_2 emissions data are available up to 2007. For non-CO_2 emissions (such as methane and nitrous oxide), these data are only available up to 2005 and are not available for all countries. In addition, for some countries, their emissions data from land use, land-use change and forestry activities are also not available. However, the CAIT database contains the most up-to-date and comprehensive information found. As a result, the emissions data for 2005, which is the year with the most comprehensive record of all GHG emissions for all countries, will be used.

For ease of analysis, countries will also be divided into four categories, representing the emission reduction potential of each category: 1 billion tonnes and over (very high); 100 million to 1 billion tonnes (high); 10 million to 100 million tonnes (medium); and under 10 million tonnes (low). The actual GHG emissions values are contained in Appendix C.

Table 6.2 Eligible developing countries and their GHG emission reduction potential

Very high (4)	High (3)	Medium (2)	Low (1)
China	Mexico	Turkmenistan	Tajikistan
Brazil	Republic of Korea	Guatemala	Kyrgyzstan
Indonesia	Iran	Kuwait	Equatorial Guinea
India	Nigeria	Chile	Albania
	South Africa	Israel	Georgia
	Saudi Arabia	Ethiopia	Mauritania
	Malaysia	Syria	Armenia
	Thailand	Libya	Niger
	Argentina	Zimbabwe	Malawi
	Congo DR	Honduras	Togo
	Myanmar	Serbia & Montenegro	Guyana
	Pakistan	Morocco	Eritrea
	Egypt	Qatar	Solomon Islands
	Philippines	Papua New Guinea	Rwanda
	Bolivia	Oman	Mauritius
	Uzbekistan	Singapore	Sierra Leone
	Vietnam	Azerbaijan	Suriname
	Colombia	Uruguay	Fiji
	Zambia	Kenya	Swaziland

continued . . .

3   See http://mdgs.un.org/unsd/mdg/SeriesDetail.aspx?srid=749&crid= 'Carbon dioxide emissions (CO_2), thousand metric tons of CO_2 (CDIAC)' (UN MDGS, accessed 25 March 2013).

Table 6.2 Continued

Very high (4)	High (3)	Medium (2)	Low (1)
	United Arab Emirates	Cuba	Burundi
	Peru	Nepal	Bahamas
	Bangladesh	Trinidad & Tobago	Guinea-Bissau
	Algeria	Tunisia	Liberia
	Angola	Côte d'Ivoire	Bhutan
	Ecuador	Madagascar	Timor-Leste
	Sudan	Uganda	Lesotho
	Iraq	Mongolia	Barbados
	Democratic People's Republic of Korea	Yemen	Gambia
	Tanzania	Paraguay	Djibouti
	Cambodia	Dominican Republic	Belize
	Cameroon	Sri Lanka	Haiti
		Mozambique	Maldives
		Jordan	Cape Verde
		Mali	Antigua & Barbuda
		Senegal	Saint Lucia
		Ghana	Samoa
		Bahrain	Grenada
		Chad	Comoros
		Bosnia & Herzegovina	São Tomé & Principe
		Lebanon	
		Guinea	
		Burkina Faso	
		Lao	
		Gabon	
		Nicaragua	
		Moldova	
		Jamaica	
		Botswana	
		Namibia	
		Macedonia	
		Benin	
		El Salvador	
		Panama	
		Costa Rica	

Source of data: CAIT Version 7.0 (2005).
Source of classification: Author.

6.3 CDM potential and the current geographic distribution of projects

Having classified countries according to their emission reduction potential and their need, this book now shows the complete CDM potential of all countries. To do this, a simple arithmetic calculation is done using the values assigned to each country grouping in Tables 6.1 and 6.2, and adding these numbers to show overall, out of 8, what each country's potential is.

Countries are then classified again into four groups, to show what the distribution of projects among countries should look like, based on their CDM potential. The categories and values used are as follows: very high CDM potential (7–8); high CDM potential (5–6); medium CDM potential (3–4); and low CDM potential (1–2). This is compared with the current geographic distribution of projects, to show whether or not this distribution is equitable. This is presented in Table 6.3 opposite.

The first point to note about this table is that it is intended as a rough representation of countries' CDM potential. It cannot, and is not intended to, be used to determine exactly how many projects countries should host compared with other countries. Instead, the purpose of Table 6.3 is to provide a guide as to which countries should be performing well under the CDM, owing to both their emission reduction potential and need taken together. The ultimate objective is to use this information to reach a conclusion about whether or not those countries that should be doing well are the ones doing well, and, if not, to ascertain the possible reasons for this. However, the exact number of projects that a particular country can or should host will depend on the country's own emission reduction potential and need.

This is particularly so because, owing to countries' varying emission reduction potential, the number of projects they can host will also vary. Therefore, countries that, according to Table 6.3, have the same CDM potential are not necessarily expected to host the same number of projects. For example, although Guinea-Bissau and Iran have the same CDM potential value of 7, this does not mean both countries should host the same number of projects. Whereas Guinea-Bissau has a low emission reduction potential, Iran has a high potential, and this necessarily affects the numbers of projects these countries can host. This, however, does not change the fact that Guinea-Bissau should be performing well under the CDM because it has a high CDM potential, considering both its emission reduction potential and need. Because Guinea-Bissau has high need, it should receive priority (preferential treatment) to facilitate its participation in the CDM and to enable it to achieve the emission reduction potential that it does have. However, the precise meaning of 'well', in terms of exact number of projects, will depend on the country's emission reduction potential and how many projects it can physically host. And because the country currently hosts no

Table 6.3 Current geographic distribution of projects compared with ideal distribution/prioritisation of hosting

	Country	Potential	Need	CDM potential	No. of registered projects
1	Angola	High (3)	Very high (4)	Very high (7)	0
2	Bangladesh	High (3)	Very high (4)	Very high (7)	2
3	Cameroon	High (3)	Very high (4)	Very high (7)	2
4	China	Very high (4)	High (3)	Very high (7)	3,480
5	Congo DR	High (3)	Very high (4)	Very high (7)	2
6	India	Very high (4)	High (3)	Very high (7)	1,197
7	Indonesia	Very high (4)	High (3)	Very high (7)	124
8	Myanmar	High (3)	Very high (4)	Very high (7)	0
9	Nigeria	High (3)	Very high (4)	Very high (7)	7
10	Pakistan	High (3)	Very high (4)	Very high (7)	23
11	Sudan	High (3)	Very high (4)	Very high (7)	0
12	Tanzania	High (3)	Very high (4)	Very high (7)	2
13	Zambia	High (3)	Very high (4)	Very high (7)	1
14	Benin	Medium (2)	Very high (4)	High (6)	0
15	Bolivia	High (3)	High (3)	High (6)	4
16	Brazil	Very high (4)	Medium (2)	High (6)	269
17	Burkina Faso	Medium (2)	Very high (4)	High (6)	0
18	Cambodia	High (3)	High (3)	High (6)	8
19	Chad	Medium (2)	Very high (4)	High (6)	0
20	Côte d'Ivoire	Medium (2)	Very high (4)	High (6)	4
21	Egypt	High (3)	High (3)	High (6)	13
22	Ethiopia	Medium (2)	Very high (4)	High (6)	1
23	Guinea	Medium (2)	Very high (4)	High (6)	0
24	Iraq	High (3)	High (3)	High (6)	0
25	Kenya	Medium (2)	Very high (4)	High (6)	14
26	Madagascar	Medium (2)	Very high (4)	High (6)	3
27	Mali	Medium (2)	Very high (4)	High (6)	1
28	Mozambique	Medium (2)	Very high (4)	High (6)	0
29	Nepal	Medium (2)	Very high (4)	High (6)	2
30	Papua New Guinea	Medium (2)	Very high (4)	High (6)	7
31	Philippines	High (3)	High (3)	High (6)	62
32	Senegal	Medium (2)	Very high (4)	High (6)	4
33	South Africa	High (3)	High (3)	High (6)	40
34	Thailand	High (3)	High (3)	High (6)	114
35	Uganda	Medium (2)	Very high (4)	High (6)	12
36	Uzbekistan	High (3)	High (3)	High (6)	14
37	Vietnam	High (3)	High (3)	High (6)	231
38	Yemen	Medium (2)	Very high (4)	High (6)	0
39	Zimbabwe	Medium (2)	Very high (4)	High (6)	1
40	Algeria	High (3)	Medium (2)	High (5)	2
41	Botswana	Medium (2)	High (3)	High (5)	0
42	Burundi	Low (1)	Very high (4)	High (5)	0
43	Colombia	High (3)	Medium (2)	High (5)	46
44	Comoros	Low (1)	Very high (4)	High (5)	0
45	Djibouti	Low (1)	Very high (4)	High (5)	0

continued . . .

Table 6.3 Continued

	Country	Potential	Need	CDM potential	No. of registered projects
46	Dominican Republic	Medium (2)	High (3)	High (5)	11
47	Ecuador	High (3)	Medium (2)	High (5)	21
48	El Salvador	Medium (2)	High (3)	High (5)	6
49	Eritrea	Low (1)	Very high (4)	High (5)	0
50	Gabon	Medium (2)	High (3)	High (5)	0
51	Gambia	Low (1)	Very high (4)	High (5)	0
52	Ghana	Medium (2)	High (3)	High (5)	1
53	Guatemala	Medium (2)	High (3)	High (5)	15
54	Guinea-Bissau	Low (1)	Very high (4)	High (5)	0
55	Haiti	Low (1)	Very high (4)	High (5)	0
56	Honduras	Medium (2)	High (3)	High (5)	25
57	Iran	High (3)	Medium (2)	High (5)	12
58	Jordan	Medium (2)	High (3)	High (5)	4
59	Lao	Medium (2)	High (3)	High (5)	5
60	Lesotho	Low (1)	Very high (4)	High (5)	1
61	Liberia	Low (1)	Very high (4)	High (5)	1
62	Malawi	Low (1)	Very high (4)	High (5)	0
63	Malaysia	High (3)	Medium (2)	High (5)	131
64	Mauritania	Low (1)	Very high (4)	High (5)	0
65	Mexico	High (3)	Medium (2)	High (5)	171
66	Moldova	Medium (2)	High (3)	High (5)	6
67	Mongolia	Medium (2)	High (3)	High (5)	4
68	Morocco	Medium (2)	High (3)	High (5)	11
69	Namibia	Medium (2)	High (3)	High (5)	1
70	Nicaragua	Medium (2)	High (3)	High (5)	9
71	Niger	Low (1)	Very high (4)	High (5)	0
72	Paraguay	Medium (2)	High (3)	High (5)	2
73	Peru	High (3)	Medium (2)	High (5)	49
74	Rwanda	Low (1)	Very high (4)	High (5)	4
75	São Tomé & Principe	Low (1)	Very high (4)	High (5)	0
76	Saudi Arabia	High (3)	Medium (2)	High (5)	2
77	Sierra Leone	Low (1)	Very high (4)	High (5)	0
78	Solomon Islands	Low (1)	Very high (4)	High (5)	0
79	Syria	Medium (2)	High (3)	High (5)	2
80	Togo	Low (1)	Very high (4)	High (5)	0
81	Turkmenistan	Medium (2)	High (3)	High (5)	0
82	Antigua & Barbuda	Low (1)	Medium (2)	Medium (4)	0
83	Bhutan	Low (1)	High (3)	Medium (4)	2
84	Bosnia & Herzegovina	Medium (2)	Medium (2)	Medium (4)	2
85	Libya	Medium (2)	Medium (2)	Medium (4)	1
86	Oman	Medium (2)	Medium (2)	Medium (4)	0
87	Swaziland	Low (1)	High (3)	Medium (4)	0

continued . . .

Table 6.3 Continued

	Country	Potential	Need	CDM potential	No. of registered projects
88	Timor-Leste	Low (1)	High (3)	Medium (4)	0
89	Argentina	High (3)	Low (1)	Medium (4)	35
90	Azerbaijan	Medium (2)	Medium (2)	Medium (4)	4
91	Bahrain	Medium (2)	Medium (2)	Medium (4)	0
92	Belize	Low (1)	High (3)	Medium (4)	0
93	Cape Verde	Low (1)	High (3)	Medium (4)	0
94	Costa Rica	Medium (2)	Medium (2)	Medium (4)	13
95	Cuba	Medium (2)	Medium (2)	Medium (4)	2
96	Equatorial Guinea	Low (1)	High (3)	Medium (4)	0
97	Fiji	Low (1)	High (3)	Medium (4)	2
98	Guyana	Low (1)	High (3)	Medium (4)	1
99	Jamaica	Medium (2)	Medium (2)	Medium (4)	2
100	Republic of Korea	High (3)	Low (1)	Medium (4)	86
101	Kuwait	Medium (2)	Medium (2)	Medium (4)	0
102	Kyrgyzstan	Low (1)	High (3)	Medium (4)	0
103	Lebanon	Medium (2)	Medium (2)	Medium (4)	5
104	Macedonia	Medium (2)	Medium (2)	Medium (4)	4
105	Maldives	Low (1)	High (3)	Medium (4)	0
106	Montenegro	Medium (2)	Medium (2)	Medium (4)	0
107	Panama	Medium (2)	Medium (2)	Medium (4)	13
108	Samoa	Low (1)	High (3)	Medium (4)	0
109	Serbia	Medium (2)	Medium (2)	Medium (4)	6
110	Sri Lanka	Medium (2)	Medium (2)	Medium (4)	9
111	Suriname	Low (1)	High (3)	Medium (4)	0
112	Tajikistan	Low (1)	High (3)	Medium (4)	0
113	Trinidad & Tobago	Medium (2)	Medium (2)	Medium (4)	0
114	Tunisia	Medium (2)	Medium (2)	Medium (4)	5
115	United Arab Emirates	High (3)	Low (1)	Medium (4)	11
116	Uruguay	Medium (2)	Medium (2)	Medium (4)	17
117	Albania	Low (1)	Medium (2)	Medium (3)	3
118	Armenia	Low (1)	Medium (2)	Medium (3)	6
119	Bahamas	Low (1)	Medium (2)	Medium (3)	1
120	Chile	Medium (2)	Low (1)	Medium (3)	78
121	Georgia	Low (1)	Medium (2)	Medium (3)	5
122	Grenada	Low (1)	Medium (2)	Medium (3)	0
123	Israel	Medium (2)	Low (1)	Medium (3)	29
124	Mauritius	Low (1)	Medium (2)	Medium (3)	2
125	Qatar	Medium (2)	Low (1)	Medium (3)	1
126	Saint Lucia	Low (1)	Medium (2)	Medium (3)	0
127	Singapore	Medium (2)	Low (1)	Medium (3)	3
128	Barbados	Low (1)	Low (1)	Low (2)	0
129	Korea DPR	High (3)	NA	NA	6

Source: Author.
Source of project data: CDM Pipeline (1 March 2013).

projects, and the CDM is only reducing about 1.36 per cent of developing country emissions, it is obvious that the country can, and should, do much better than it is currently doing.

The scale of the projects hosted, whether large or small scale, also affects the number of projects a country can host. One single large-scale project can reduce the same amount of GHG emissions as several small-scale projects, and, therefore, when determining how many projects countries can or should host, the size or scale of the projects also plays an important role. However, this detail is not provided in Table 6.3, because it is not relevant to the information the table aims to present – the aim is not to specify how many projects countries should host, but to identify countries' CDM potential and also to identify those countries doing well under the CDM and those not doing well.

Considering that all countries produce GHG emissions and, therefore, all have the potential to reduce their GHG emissions, but the CDM is only reducing about 1.36 per cent of total developing country emissions, generally, all countries have the potential to host more projects. However, as already explained, to determine the exact number of projects a particular country should host, its emission reduction potential (with necessary deductions made for the volume of emissions already being reduced through the CDM and other means, if any) will require to be taken into consideration.

6.4 Analysis of the geographic distribution of CDM projects

Table 6.3 shows clearly the countries with the highest CDM potential. Thirteen countries have very high CDM potential, and a further sixty-eight have high potential (eighty-one in total). Within these categories are those hosting the largest number of projects (such as India, China, Vietnam and Brazil), and this is as it should be. On the other hand, out of these eighty-one countries, fifty-four currently host projects, but this hosting is extremely skewed. It ranges from China hosting 3,480 projects to countries such as Mali and Ghana hosting 1. The other twenty-seven countries, such as Myanmar, Benin and Iraq, host no projects at all.

This skewed distribution cannot be explained solely by the GHG emission reduction potential of countries. Although the countries that are currently performing well are among those with the highest GHG emission reduction potential (such as China, Brazil, Indonesia, India and Vietnam), many of the countries that also have relatively high potential are underperforming (such as Angola and Myanmar with no projects, and Bangladesh and Cameroon with 2 projects each), particularly when compared with other countries in the same category (such as Indonesia with 124 projects and Colombia with 46) or those in a lower category (such as Chile with 78 projects and Israel with 29). Therefore, the current distribution of projects cannot be justified on the basis of countries' emission reduction potential.

It also cannot be explained by countries' need, as the current distribution of CDM projects does not match with that required by the element of need. The groups of countries with the greatest need (such as those with high and very high need, shown in Table 6.1) are actually hosting the least number of projects, with most of them not hosting any project. Therefore, considering both GHG emission reduction potential and need separately, neither of these elements explains the current distribution of CDM projects.

Also taking both indicators together, the distribution of projects is still inequitable. Not only are many of the countries with the highest CDM potential underperforming (such as Angola, Myanmar, Sudan, Iraq and Yemen), Table 6.3 in fact shows that many of the countries (such as Chile, Mexico, Malaysia, Colombia, Israel and the Republic of Korea) currently performing very well under the CDM are not those with the very highest CDM potential. In fact, countries such as Israel and Chile have among the lowest CDM potential, but a relatively high number of projects. This again cannot be explained by either their GHG emission reduction potential (just medium) or their need (low). In relation to those countries with higher CDM potential, the conclusion must be that this distribution is not equitable.

It is, therefore, reasonable to conclude, based on the data set out above, that the current geographic distribution of CDM projects is inequitable.

6.5 Conclusion

This chapter examined the current distribution of projects among countries with the aim of determining whether this distribution is equitable or inequitable. The conclusion reached is that it is inequitable. The current distribution cannot be explained by countries' GHG emission reduction potential, because many countries with relatively high levels of GHG emissions are underperforming, whereas some countries with relatively low GHG emission levels are performing well under the CDM. Likewise, the current distribution cannot be explained by countries' need, because most of the countries with the highest need are underperforming, whereas some countries with the lowest levels of need are actually doing well under the CDM. Consequently, the conclusion is that the distribution is inequitable, and the reason for this inequity cannot be found solely in countries' emission reduction potential or need.

In order to address the problem of the inequitable geographic distribution of projects, it is necessary to ascertain the cause(s) of the problem, so that efforts can be targeted at these causes. This is the focus of Part III.

Part III

Achieving equitable distribution

Part II of this book focused on defining distributive justice within the CDM, a task necessary to provide a 'goalpost' for all the efforts towards achieving equitable distribution. It defined equitable distribution as requiring full consideration of countries' emission reduction potential and need, and ascertained that the current distribution of projects is inequitable. Following on from these conclusions, this part focuses on what can be done to address this situation. It does this, first, by identifying the main challenges to achieving equitable distribution and then making recommendations on how these challenges can be overcome. It concludes by showing that, by further regulating the CDM regime, it is possible to achieve a more equitable distribution of projects among developing countries.

7 Barriers to equitable distribution

Part I

The current distribution of projects under the CDM is inequitable. This fact is clearly demonstrated in Chapter 6. Although many of the countries with the greatest CDM potential are doing very well in terms of project hosting, many are not. And many of the countries that are doing well are among those with the least potential. What are the reasons for this inequity? This is the question this chapter seeks to answer.

Specifically, this chapter examines the current CDM regime to determine the barriers to the equitable distribution of CDM projects and identify the primary reasons for the current inequitable distribution of projects. It shows that there are several reasons why certain countries or groups of countries have been unable to attract CDM investment, reasons such as lack of capacity and lack of funding to cover the project transaction costs. It concludes, however, that the two main reasons for the skewed distribution of projects are the unilateral CDM structure and the market-based nature of the mechanism itself. These two reasons have resulted in the CDM being flooded with CDM projects from a select few countries, rather than a wide spread of countries, as it should be.

Some of the barriers to participation in the CDM and to equitable distribution of projects are internal to the countries involved, and include barriers that would affect any kind of investment. Examples of such internal barriers are corruption, lack of security, poor governance structures, conflict and political instability, all of which lead to high investment risks (Globerman and Shapiro 2002; Habib and Zurawicki 2002; Dupasquier and Osakwe 2006; Busse and Hefeker 2007). These internal barriers to investment are beyond the scope of the CDM regime, and so will not be discussed in this chapter, because modifications to the CDM regime itself at the international level cannot address these barriers. However, many other barriers stem from the institutional makeup of the CDM itself and are issues that the international CDM regime can address, such as lack of capacity and lack of financing opportunities. These CDM barriers are the focus of this chapter.

Nevertheless, before moving on, it is important to show that these internal barriers are not the key or sole reasons for the inequitable distribution of

CDM projects. This is because, if the distribution of projects is primarily inequitable because of these internal barriers, and, as noted above, the CDM regime cannot by itself address these barriers, then the conclusion would have to be that the CDM regime cannot address the problem of inequitable distribution of projects.

Statistics show that, although many countries do have internal barriers to investment, this has not stopped some of them from performing well under the CDM. In addition, some of the countries that are actually doing well in terms of their internal governance structures are underperforming under the CDM.

For instance, Botswana, Namibia, Cape Verde, Mauritius and Uruguay are performing relatively well in terms of the World Bank's governance indicators,[1] which are: voice and accountability, political stability and absence of violence, government effectiveness, regulatory quality, rule of law and control of corruption.[2] Nevertheless, these countries are not doing very well under the CDM: Botswana and Cape Verde do not host any projects; Namibia hosts one; Mauritius hosts two; and Uruguay hosts seventeen. The Republic of Korea, whose good governance ranking is similar to these countries', hosts eighty-six projects.

Most countries have much worse rankings than these – in general, the governance rankings of most developing countries are not particularly high. Mexico, Brazil and Malaysia have slightly worse rankings, and they host 171, 269 and 131 projects, respectively. The Philippines, Thailand and Vietnam have much worse rankings, but they host 62, 114 and 231 projects, respectively. China, which hosts over half of all registered projects (3,480), ranks much lower compared with many other countries, such as Brazil (269), South Africa (40), Bhutan (2) and Lesotho (1), but this has not stopped it from being the single largest CDM host country and doing far better than these other countries.

Even though some of these differences can be explained by the varying levels of emission reduction potential and/or need in these countries, not all can. For example, South Africa has more emission reduction potential and greater need than Thailand,[3] and South Africa's governance ranking by the World Bank is higher than that of Thailand, but, whereas South Africa hosts 40 projects, Thailand hosts almost three times that number – 114 projects.[4]

---

1 For the World Bank good governance indicators, see http://info.worldbank.org/governance/wgi/index.asp 'The Worldwide Governance Indicators (WGI) project' (World Bank, 22 March 2011).
2 These countries are performing well for most, though not necessarily all, of the indicators. But, in comparison with other developing countries, they *are* performing very well.
3 In absolute values. See Appendixes A and B for countries' GHG emission reduction and HDI values. In the classification in Chapter 6, both have the same emission reduction potential and need rankings (as these rankings cover a range of values).

These statistics suggest that, although internal structures and barriers probably play a part in determining the distribution of CDM projects, there are other, probably more important, considerations that investors look out for, and these internal barriers are not the overriding barrier to CDM participation. Therefore, this chapter determines what the other barriers to equitable distribution are and also identifies the key barriers to equitable distribution, arising from the CDM regime itself.

7.1 Lack of capacity and local expertise

There are two different elements to hosting CDM projects that may impact on the equitable distribution of projects: the CDM-specific element and the general investment/project element. CDM-specific issues arise out of the need to comply with the various CDM modalities and procedures when developing and implementing CDM projects.[5] These modalities and procedures relate to activities such as selecting and applying baseline methodologies to establish baselines, proving additionality and preparing the necessary project documentation such as the project design documents (PDDs), as well as other issues such as an effective DNA, general CDM awareness and willingness to participate in the CDM.

General investment issues are those that would affect normal investments (not just CDM projects) and relate to the underlying project.[6] They include the legal and regulatory framework for investment within the host developing country, political stability and adequate infrastructure, such as transportation and telecommunications facilities. Lack of capacity in these two areas (that is, lack of CDM-specific and general investment capacity) has been identified as one of the barriers to CDM hosting and equitable

---

4 All governance statistics are for 2011 (the latest available) and are available at http://info.worldbank.org/governance/wgi/sc_country.asp 'Access governance indicators' (World Bank, 23 March 2011). Even computing beyond 2011, the conclusion remains that governance is not the key barrier to equitable distribution. For example, comparing South Africa's and the Philippines' governance indicators for 2008–2010, South Africa has consistently ranked higher, but Thailand is still performing better under the CDM.

5 The rules relating to the CDM are provided by the COP/MOP and the CDM Executive Board. The basic rules can be found in the early decisions of the COP/MOP: Decision 3/CMP.1, 'CDM modalities and procedures'; Decision 5/CMP.1, 'Modalities and procedures for CDM afforestation and reforestation project activities in the first commitment period of the Kyoto Protocol'; and Decision 6/CMP.1, 'Simplified modalities and procedures for small-scale afforestation and reforestation project activities under the CDM in the first commitment period of the Kyoto Protocol and measures to facilitate their implementation.' In addition to these, there are various other rules that must be complied with by project developers and other project participants.

6 CDM projects are essentially standard or typical projects with added CDM elements, so, for instance, issues affecting or relevant to a standard hydropower project would also affect a CDM hydropower project.

distribution of projects (Boyd *et al.* 2007: 23; Lutzeyer 2008: 27; Prouty 2009: 523).

However, this section focuses on the CDM-specific capacity issues, because, as noted above, this chapter focuses on the barriers that stem from the CDM's institutional make-up, as it is these that the CDM regime can effectively address. Issues such as political stability and regulatory and business transparency go beyond what the CDM regime can address, and, in any case, as noted above, are probably not the key barriers to equitable distribution of CDM projects.

Regarding lack of CDM capacity as a barrier to CDM development, the CDM framework within host countries is clearly an important factor that can help or hinder CDM project development (Ellis and Kamel 2007: 25). This is because the various elements of CDM project development and implementation can be fairly technical and complicated and require a degree of expertise to act within the rules. Specifically, lack of CDM capacity has been identified as a barrier to CDM development in some groups of countries, such as LDCs and African countries. Many of these countries lack: the capacity to conduct project baseline studies and fulfil approved methodologies (owing to a lack of local infrastructure and qualified personnel); CDM knowledge at the project origination level (that is, among those that should ordinarily originate projects, such as rural electrification and solid waste management practitioners); and adequate CDM information among financial intermediaries (Ellis and Kamel 2007: 25, 29–30; Oppenoorth *et al.* 2007: 18; Lutzeyer 2008: 27).

One point to be made is that the real barrier to equitable distribution might be a *perception* of lack of capacity, rather than an actual lack of capacity. This is because there does not appear to have been any comprehensive study of the technical capacity of all developing countries to host CDM projects. Although there is some information available about the general investment climate in many countries, this information is either not comprehensive or does not cover all countries.

For example, the World Bank's good governance indicators do not specifically cover technical capacity in a comprehensive manner, even though they could help with the evaluation of countries' general investment climate. Even the World Bank's Investment Climate Assessments have only been carried out for some developing countries and mostly do not assess CDM capacity – although they cover the general investment climate in these countries.[7]

---

7 See the World Bank's Investment Climate Assessments. Online. Available at: www-wds. worldbank.org/external/default/main?menuPK=64187282&pagePK=64187835&piPK=64 187936&theSitePK=523679&sType=2&author=&aType=2&docTitle=&tType=2&doc Type=3&fromDate=&toDate=&region=119222&cntry=&topic=&lang=&=&docTY=904 594&lndinstr=&prdln=&report=&loan=&credit=&projectId=&trustFunds=&sortDesc=D

Therefore, although this book does not dispute that many countries probably lack sufficient capacity to register and implement CDM projects, it emphasises the need for a comprehensive study to determine countries' capacity to enable targeted and effective capacity building to be undertaken.

Lack of capacity, particularly project development capacity, constitutes a barrier to CDM hosting and the equitable distribution of projects, primarily because of the unilateral nature of many CDM projects.[8] In the unilateral CDM structure, developing country entities develop and implement projects themselves, rather than with developed country support, as was originally envisaged. As a result of this, those that lack the capacity to develop and implement projects are underperforming in the CDM market, which is currently dominated by unilateral projects.

In addition, it must be noted that one of the objectives of the CDM, as already discussed, is to promote sustainable development, and the CDM is, inter alia, expected to facilitate technology transfer and capacity building in developing countries. Particularly in relation to the ability to actually implement CDM projects, current inability or limited ability to do so should not constitute a reason for not implementing CDM projects in these countries. On the contrary, it should be seen as a measure of their sustainable development potential, and such technical capacity should be built through both capacity building and 'learning-by-doing'.

It cannot, however, be denied that many countries lack sufficient capacity to develop and implement CDM projects compared with other countries, and that this negatively impacts on their attractiveness to CDM investors. This capacity barrier to equitable distribution of CDM projects primarily undermines the 'need' factor for achieving equitable distribution, because the countries with the lowest human development and greatest need are often those with the least capacity and expertise. It also undermines the 'potential' factor, because many of the countries that lack the capacity to effectively participate in the CDM and are, therefore, affected by this capacity barrier, such as LDCs and sub-Saharan African countries among others, do have sufficient emission reduction potential to participate in the CDM.

Recognising that lack of capacity is a barrier to CDM hosting, various international organisations have capacity-building programmes aimed at enhancing countries' CDM capacity. For example, UNEP's Capacity Development for the Clean Development Mechanism (CD4CDM) project was established to build developing country capacity to participate in the

---

OCDT&sortType=0&pageSize=50&pageSize=50&pageSize=50&dAtts=DOCDT,DOCNA,REPNB,DOCTY,LANG,VOLNB,REPNME (World Bank, 26 January 2010).

8 See the discussion below of the unilateral CDM structure as a barrier to equitable distribution. See Chapter 2 for a discussion of the CDM structure, including the unilateral, bilateral and multilateral CDM structures.

CDM, and the project organises training workshops and publishes CDM guidebooks to help achieve this objective (UNEP CD4CDM). Other institutions and (developed) countries also provide capacity building to developing countries to build their CDM capacity, both within and outside the CDM framework.[9] In addition to these external programmes, several initiatives have been launched within the CDM framework to build developing countries' capacity to host projects. These initiatives are examined in Chapter 9, and the extent to which they have succeeded in their goal of building CDM capacity is also analysed.

7.2 Cost-related barriers

Lack of funding is considered to be a major barrier to the equitable distribution of CDM projects, or as a barrier to the hosting of projects by certain groups of countries, such as LDCs and African countries (UNEP and Ecosecurities 2007: 3, 7). As with most projects, the funding required for CDM projects can be divided into funding for the project transaction costs and funding for the underlying project.

7.2.1 Transaction costs

Transaction costs are costs that accrue in the process of making an economic exchange or effecting a transfer of goods from seller to buyer. Although there is no generally accepted definition, transaction costs have been defined as the 'costs of running the economic system' (Pitelis 1993: 9) or the costs of organising and conducting business activities (Holden 2004: 1).

Under the CDM, transaction costs are incurred in the creation, alteration, protection or enforcement of CERs and have been described as additional costs beyond the cost of production (UNDP 2003: 56). These include the

---

9 For example, the Institute for Global Environmental Strategies (IGES), established by an initiative of the Japanese Government, runs the CDM Programme, which provides CDM capacity building to developing countries in Asia. See 'Market mechanism (CDM programme)' at: www.iges.or.jp/en/cdm/index.html (IGES, 26 January 2010). For a description of the various capacity-building activities undertaken by the UN Industrial Development Organization (UNIDO), see *CDM Project Activities/Capacity Building*. Online. Available at: www.unido.org/what-we-do/environment/energy-access-for-productive-uses/industrial-energy-efficiency/selected-projects/kyoto-protocol-and-clean-development-mechanisms-cdm/cdm-project-activities.html (UNIDO, 9 February 2010). The World Bank's Carbon Finance Assist programme is a 'consolidated capacity building and technical assistance' programme that aims to enhance capacity and expertise of host countries to participate in the CDM, inter alia. See 'Capacity building' at: http://web.worldbank.org/WBSITE/EXTERNAL/TOPICS/ENVIRONMENT/EXTCARBONFINANCE/0,,contentMDK:21849454~menuPK:5232931~pagePK:64168445~piPK:64168309~theSitePK:4125853,00.html (World Bank, 9 February 2010).

cost of identifying potential CDM projects, identifying potential partners and negotiating the CDM contract, the costs involved in the approval process, such as those associated with establishing baselines, proving additionality, validation, registration and verification of the project, as well as the share of proceeds and registration fees required by the Protocol. These are CDM project transaction costs, as they do not result directly from implementing the CDM projects themselves.

Transaction costs constitute a barrier to CDM project development by local developers who do not have, and cannot raise, the funds required to pay project transaction costs. As these costs are incurred upfront before projects generate CERs, project developers would require some financing to cover the costs, which could be quite substantial (Ellis and Kamel 2007: 33). UNEP estimates the costs incurred during the planning phase as US$18,500–610,000, depending on various things such as the complexity and scale of the project (UNEP and Ecosecurities 2007: 56).

Generally, host country project developers are only required to bear the bulk of these transaction costs in the case of unilateral projects, where the host country entity itself undertakes and finances all the preliminary elements of the CDM project. However, even in the case of bilateral projects, host country project developers may still have to bear some of the transaction costs, such as negotiation costs.

In order to address this problem, some CER purchasers offer advance payments to project developers to help them pay the project transaction costs. This advance payment could be in the form of an advance payment of the purchase price of the CERs (Ellis and Kamel 2007: 32–33; UNEP and Ecosecurities 2007: 56). For example, the World Bank states that it can advance funds for the preparation of the necessary CDM documentation and recover the costs of preparing the documentation from future payments. It also states it can make upfront payments of up to 25 per cent of the value of the purchase contract.[10]

Transaction costs are also a barrier to equitable distribution, when high transaction costs associated with investment in some countries discourage investors from investing in such countries. As noted by the UNDP, if the transaction costs associated with the CDM project are high compared with the total costs of the project, this reduces the project's feasibility (UNDP 2003: 57). This is also of concern in the case of small-scale projects, which do not generate large quantities of CERs, compared with large-scale projects, as 'the smaller the project's financing requirements, the higher

---

10 See 'For project developers' at: http://web.worldbank.org/WBSITE/EXTERNAL/TOPICS/ENVIRONMENT/EXTCARBONFINANCE/0,,contentMDK:21844272~menuPK:5220636~pagePK:64168445~piPK:64168309~theSitePK:4125853,00.html (World Bank, 3 February 2010).

the financing transaction costs per unit of finance will be' (UNEP and Ecosecurities 2007: 75).

High transaction costs could also act as a barrier where the transaction costs of projects are higher in some areas and for some projects than others. This constitutes a barrier in cases where the foreign entity actually invests in the CDM project directly, rather than just purchasing the CERs generated from the project. Where the foreign entity is only purchasing CERs generated (as with CERs generated by unilateral projects), most of the transaction costs are borne by the project developer and would not impact on the investor. In addition, to the extent that high transaction costs would drive up the price of CERs, this could also affect the attractiveness of such CERs to investors, especially considering the market nature of the CDM, where host countries are competing for CERs, and investors can simply purchase CERs from other projects if the price for the CERs generated by some projects is too high.

This transaction costs barrier to equitable distribution of CDM projects particularly affects those countries with the greatest need and therefore undermines the 'need' factor for achieving equitable distribution (Michaelowa 2005: 11–13; Ellis and Kamel 2007: 32–33). It also obviously undermines the 'potential' factor, because some of these countries with the greatest need, which are unable to effectively participate in the CDM, also have emission reduction potential. Their inability to participate effectively means that their potential is not being adequately exploited under the CDM.

In order to address the problem of the transaction costs of small-scale projects (by reducing such transaction costs), the CDM Executive Board has adopted simplified modalities and procedures for small-scale CDM project activities (Decisions 17/CP.7 and 4/CMP.1) and simplified baseline and monitoring methodologies for small-scale afforestation and reforestation project activities (Decision 7/CMP.1, paragraph 3). These initiatives are discussed in Chapter 9.

7.2.2 Implementation costs

These refer to the actual costs of implementing projects, rather than the costs associated with organising production. Under the CDM, the implementation costs are the direct costs of the activities that lead to either removing a GHG from the atmosphere or preventing the emission of the GHG to the atmosphere. These would include the project construction costs (such as purchasing or constructing the plant and equipment) and the project operation costs (such as the cost of maintenance and other running costs). For example, the implementation costs of a CDM hydropower project would include the cost of constructing and operating the hydropower station, but, as already noted above, would exclude the costs involved in registering the project with the CDM Executive Board. Generally, the largest costs associated with a project are implementation costs, incurred specifically at the construction stage. UNEP estimates that even a relatively small engineering project could cost several million dollars (UNEP and Ecosecurities 2007: 29).

Lack of finance for the project itself has been identified as a major barrier to CDM participation, particularly for those smaller developing countries that do not have strong financial institutions, such as many LDCs and African countries (Ellis and Kamel 2007: 30–32; UNEP and Ecosecurities 2007: 3, 7; Sieghart 2009: 201).

The original expectation from the CDM was that it would attract foreign direct investment in CDM projects, beyond the purchase of CERs generated by the projects. If this original expectation was generally the case, local project developers would only have to secure foreign investment in projects in exchange for the CERs generated by the project, and this investment would cover the production costs of the projects. However, because of the prevalence of unilateral CDM projects and pure CER purchase-type agreements, the norm has become that local developers need to source local financing for the projects and then secure foreign developed country counterparts to purchase the CERs generated by the projects.

This is a problem for many countries that do not have well-developed financial institutions, as well as for those where, although such institutions exist, local financiers are reluctant to invest in CDM projects because of a lack of understanding of the CDM's operation and because of the greater risk compared with other kinds of project. In these situations, local developers have difficulty obtaining the required financing for the projects locally and depend on foreign investment, which is often not forthcoming because of the preference for simply purchasing CERs.

For example, the World Bank states that it will not provide debt and/or equity finance for the baseline component of projects, which should be financed by other sources, but will pay on delivery of CERs.[11] However, it can pay up to 25 per cent of the CER purchase price upfront, where it can be demonstrated that such upfront payment is necessary.[12] Although the portion of the price paid upfront is rarely sufficient to cover the implementation costs, it can contribute to paying the costs (probably only the transaction costs) and assist the project developer to obtain other financing (UNEP and Ecosecurities 2007: 69).

Just like the transaction costs barrier, this implementation costs barrier undermines the 'need' and 'potential' factors for achieving equitable

---

11 See 'Minimum project requirements' at: http://web.worldbank.org/WBSITE/EXTERNAL/ TOPICS/ENVIRONMENT/EXTCARBONFINANCE/0,,contentMDK:21844766~menuPK :5220728~pagePK:64168445~piPK:64168309~theSitePK:4125853,00.html (World Bank, 3 February 2010).

12 See 'For project developers' at: http://web.worldbank.org/WBSITE/EXTERNAL/TOPICS/ ENVIRONMENT/EXTCARBONFINANCE/0,,contentMDK:21844272~menuPK:5220636 ~pagePK:64168445~piPK:64168309~theSitePK:4125853,00.html (World Bank, 3 February 2010).

distribution of CDM projects. Unfortunately, as is explained further in Chapter 9, there are currently no initiatives under the CDM regime to address this barrier.

7.3 Preference for large-scale projects

The size of CDM projects has been identified as a barrier to the distribution of projects. Specifically, this refers to investors' preference for investing in projects that will generate a specified minimum quantity of CERs. This is partly in order to ensure that, considering the project transaction costs, the quantity of CERs generated will be sufficient to make the project worthwhile.

Linked to this barrier is the relatively low level of industrial development of some countries, resulting in limited opportunities for large-scale projects.[13] Obviously, the smaller the size of a project, the fewer CERs it will generate. Therefore, some investors prefer to invest in large projects in order to maximise economies of scale. Because the CDM is in part a mechanism to assist developed countries to meet their Kyoto targets in a cost-effective way, investors will consider cost-effectiveness in determining the attractiveness of any CDM project.

Some investors, therefore, have a minimum project size they will invest in, and will not invest in CDM projects that will not generate a specified minimum quantity of CERs. For example, the World Bank requires the volume of emission reductions to be generated from a project to be large enough to make a project viable and states that, for example, a small-scale project should generate at least 50,000 tonnes of CO_2e annually.[14]

This is a particular challenge for countries that have more opportunities for small-scale projects than for large-scale projects, owing, inter alia, to their low level of industrial development resulting in limited opportunities for large-scale projects. For example, many sub-Saharan African countries and LDCs have greater potential for small-scale, than large-scale projects (Huq 2002: 22; Ellis and Kamel 2007: 32).

Although a challenge to project hosting, this preference for large-scale projects is not an overriding barrier. Even if investors do prefer to invest in large-scale projects in order to minimise cost and maximise cost-effectiveness, small-scale projects are still being developed and registered,

---

13 Ellis and Kamel note that the majority of potential CDM projects in many host countries, particularly in sub-Saharan Africa, are within the small-scale range. See Ellis and Kamel 2007: 32.

14 See the World Bank Carbon Finance website at: http://web.worldbank.org/WBSITE/ EXTERNAL/TOPICS/ENVIRONMENT/EXTCARBONFINANCE/0,,contentMDK:21844 766~menuPK:5220728~pagePK:64168445~piPK:64168309~theSitePK:4125853,00.html (World Bank, 3 February 2010).

although not at the same rate as large-scale projects. As of 1 March 2013, out of the 6,550 registered projects, 2,494 (38 per cent) were small-scale projects, and 4,062 (62 per cent) were large scale.

A possible explanation for this is that most small-scale projects are unilateral, and the host countries themselves are almost solely responsible for the projects. This would mean that what foreign investors want does not directly affect the rate of developing and implementing such projects. Some authors consider that unilateral projects have stimulated registration of many small-scale projects that would ordinarily not be very attractive to foreign investors (Sutter 2001: 6; Cosbey *et al.* 2005: 5).

The barrier presented by many investors' preference for large-scale projects mainly undermines the 'potential' factor for achieving equitable distribution. This is because, when countries with limited opportunities for large-scale projects are ignored or overlooked, their emission reduction potential (even though this potential can only be tapped primarily through small-scale projects) is basically lost and is not exploited under the CDM. In addition, it also undermines the 'need' factor, because many of the countries with the greatest need have limited opportunities for large-scale projects and are, thereby, affected by this barrier.

All these challenges have resulted in many developing countries being unable to fully participate in the CDM, and only a few countries reaping most of the benefits from the CDM. However, a fact that has become apparent from the examination of these challenges is that many of them constitute barriers to equitable distribution of projects because of two primary factors: the CDM has a prevalence of unilateral CDM projects, and this is preventing the equitable participation of countries that lack the capacity to undertake such projects; and the CDM operates in a market, where considerations of cost and risk minimisation are predominant, and equity and sustainable development are relatively unimportant.

Therefore, the next chapter focuses on these two barriers and considers their impact on the distribution of CDM projects.

8   Barriers to equitable distribution
Part II

This chapter focuses on what this book considers to be the two fundamental reasons why the current distribution of CDM projects is so inequitable: the CDM has a prevalence of unilateral CDM projects, and this is preventing the equitable participation of countries that lack the capacity to undertake such projects; and the CDM is a market mechanism for which cost and risk minimisation are overriding considerations, and equity and sustainable development are relatively unimportant. Very importantly, it also shows that the barriers identified in Chapter 7 prevent effective participation in the CDM specifically because of these two overriding barriers.

8.1 The unilateral CDM structure

The above discussions show that many of the barriers to equitable distribution, such as lack of capacity, as well as lack of financing and other cost-related barriers, constitute barriers to equitable distribution of projects primarily because of the unilateral nature of many CDM projects. Hence, one of the major barriers to equitable distribution of CDM projects is the predominance of unilateral CDM projects in the CDM market. This is a barrier mainly because unilateral projects require the developing country hosts to have sufficient financial and technical capacity to undertake such projects, and those that lack such capacity are unable to undertake unilateral projects. They are consequently sidelined in the CDM market, which is dominated by unilateral projects.

The Kyoto Protocol defines the CDM as a mechanism under which non-Annex I parties (developing countries) will benefit from project activities resulting in CERs, and Annex I parties (developed countries) may use these CERs to comply with part of their Protocol emission reduction targets (Kyoto Protocol, Article 12.3). This definition does not identify what structure CDM projects should have.

Although the Kyoto Protocol and the CDM rules left open the question of what form the CDM should take, the CDM was originally conceived as a mechanism under which developed country entities would invest in projects in developing countries and use the CERs generated to meet their emission reduction commitments. The expectation was that the CDM would follow a mainly investment model, whereby developed country entities would provide direct investment of equity or debt in projects in developing countries (Lecocq and Ambrosi 2007: 143; Muller 2007: 3205).

After the Kyoto Protocol was agreed and during the negotiation of the rules, there was some debate about whether or not unilateral projects would be allowed under the CDM. The Executive Board formally resolved this debate at its eighteenth meeting, when it agreed that a CDM project can be registered without involvement of an Annex I Party at the registration stage.[1] This effectively permitted the registration of unilateral CDM projects and, consequently, the CDM has moved from its original conception and is now also a mechanism under which developing countries themselves implement projects and sell the CERs generated to developed country entities, which these entities can then further trade or use to meet their emission reduction commitments. In this latter model, the host developing country entity itself develops, finances and implements the CDM project, with no direct investment by a developed country entity. This model is referred to as the unilateral CDM.

In the unilateral CDM structure, the CDM project is developed and implemented by local project developers, with financing obtained usually from local investors/financial institutions, and the resulting CERs are then sold to developed countries, developed country private entities or market traders. The sale of CERs could be through a forward contract, where the agreement between buyer and seller is reached and signed even before the CERs are generated (it could even be before the project is registered), or it could happen after the CERs are generated, on the 'spot' market (Curnow and Hodes 2009: 77–8).

The key element here is that the purchaser of CERs does not invest in the underlying project – the only finance provided is for the purchase of the CERs. This is the case even though, under some forward contracts (usually referred to as emission reduction purchase agreements (ERPAs)), some purchasers will advance part of the purchase price ahead of the actual performance of the contract, usually to enable the project developer to cover the transaction costs associated with the project. These projects are still unilateral – they do not fit the description of the 'bilateral' structure envisaged under the CDM.

The main distinction between unilateral and bilateral CDM projects is that, for bilateral projects, the developed country entities provide direct investment in the underlying projects, as was originally envisaged. The unilateral structure does not provide this. Even the multilateral structure has

---

1   See Report of the Eighteenth Meeting of the CDM Executive Board (CDM-EB-18), 25 February 2005, at: http://cdm.unfccc.int/EB/018/eb18rep.pdf; www.unfccc.int (UNFCCC, 15 February 2010), paragraph 57.

turned out to be very similar to the unilateral structure, with the only distinction being that, in the multilateral structure, several developed country entities act through the fund or portfolio manager. The multilateral structure often operates in the same way as unilateral projects, as the developing country hosts usually need to source the financing for the underlying projects. The multilateral funds tend to only purchase the CERs generated, possibly with some upfront/advance payment.

An example of a bilateral project is the Zafarana Wind Power Plant Project, hosted by Egypt and financed by the Japanese government through the Japan Bank for International Cooperation (JBIC), via debt financing (loan). The CERs generated by the project were contracted to be purchased by Japan Carbon Finance, acting as JBIC's indirect financial instrument. These two Japanese entities worked in collaboration, with JBIC providing the underlying finance for the project, and Japan Carbon Finance purchasing the CERs generated by the project.[2]

An example of a unilateral CDM project is the La Gloria Hydroelectric Project, hosted by Honduras. In the PDD, the UK is identified as the Annex I Party involved, and Ecosecurities is identified as the private entity involved in the project. This, on the face of it, suggests that this was a bilateral project. However, the PDD identifies that the financing for the project was provided by two local banks in Honduras (Bamer and Ficohsa). The project, therefore, does not qualify as a bilateral project, because it was unilaterally funded by the host country itself.[3]

An example of a multilateral project is the Uganda Nile Basin Reforestation Project, hosted by Uganda. The main investor in the project was Uganda's National Forest Authority, with other Ugandan community groups also providing some investment. The National Forest Authority retained all rights to the CERs generated and entered into an ERPA for the sale of the CERs. The CER buyer was the International Bank for Reconstruction and Development, as trustee of the BioCarbon Fund. This is an example of a multilateral project (as it involved an investment fund – the BioCarbon Fund, acting on behalf of public- and private-sector participants) that was actually unilaterally funded by the host country itself.[4]

These commodity-style purchase transactions are now the most common form of CDM projects. According to the UNFCCC Secretariat, about 90 per cent of CDM projects are solely domestically financed (UNFCCC 2012: 8, 41, 48). Hence, the CDM has moved away from the envisaged foreign

2   See the PDD for the project at: http://cdm.unfccc.int/UserManagement/FileStorage/ Q1QEHEZG9WGW44Q7R6W0HYKCMNZCNF (UNFCCC, 22 July 2010), 5 and 9.
3   See the PDD for the project at: http://cdm.unfccc.int/UserManagement/FileStorage/ 1L9M8SVJ034UCQYZF7HE5P6NBTDXRO (UNFCCC, 22 July 2010), 8 and 10.
4   See the PDD for the project at: http://cdm.unfccc.int/UserManagement/FileStorage/ E3A6TBOQ9RDM0KZ47WFJH5LPCYS2GU (UNFCCC, 22 July 2010), 3.

investment and involvement-based mechanism to one that mainly involves local developers and financiers.

This dominance of unilateral CDM projects in the CDM market constitutes a barrier to equitable distribution because of the inability of many countries, particularly the poorer developing countries, to undertake such projects. In the unilateral CDM structure, the developing country host must itself raise the required funds for the underlying project, rather than the financing being provided by the developed country entity in exchange for CERs. This ability to unilaterally host projects is not in itself inequitable. On the contrary, it is beneficial to those (usually larger) developing countries that can raise the necessary financing locally and that have the capacity to unilaterally develop and implement projects, because they can, inter alia, choose which projects they want to implement and focus on projects that are in line with their national sustainable development priorities.

However, because unilateral CDM projects now dominate the CDM market, this is disadvantageous to those low-income developing countries that lack the necessary capacity to unilaterally develop and implement projects and also cannot obtain the required financing locally and rely on foreign support (Paulsson 2009: 73; Sieghart 2009: 200–2). Oppenoorth *et al.* (2007: 20) give the example of a proposed CDM project in Kenya. Owing to the upfront costs required and the risks involved, all the potential buyers approached were only willing to buy the CERs generated after project registration and implementation. The project was, therefore, not able to generate the required financing and could not be registered. In this example, had Kenya been able to raise sufficient local capital to register and implement the project unilaterally, this project would have been one additional project for it.

As noted above, the ability for countries to unilaterally develop and implement CDM projects is not in itself inequitable. Some authors consider that unilateral projects have stimulated registration of many small-scale projects that would ordinarily not be very attractive to foreign investors. Some have also suggested that unilateral projects should be promoted as a way of improving the distribution of projects, stating this would benefit those countries that would ordinarily not be able to attract bilateral investment owing, for example, to country risk or a poor investment climate within the countries (Sutter 2001: 6; Jahn *et al.* 2003: 6–7; Michaelowa 2007: 24; Cosbey *et al.* 2008: 5; Paulsson 2009: 73). The disadvantage arises specifically because both unilateral and bilateral CDM projects compete in the same market and for the same developed country entities. There is a finite demand for CDM projects/CERs – they are primarily targeted at helping to meeting developed countries' emission reduction commitments.[5]

5 For an estimate of the demand for CERs, see Kossoy and Guigon (2012).

A preference for unilateral projects over bilateral projects means that the demand for bilateral projects ultimately will be reduced, as developed countries only need a certain amount of CERs to contribute to meeting their emission reduction commitments. And, because unilateral projects currently dominate the market, the share of bilateral projects is inevitably reduced.

For example, Sieghart reports that, although there is mounting interest of the carbon community in CDM projects from Yemen, this interest is mostly limited to the purchase of CERs (Sieghart 2009: 199). This could be as a result of the fact that, for many, or even most, developed country entities participating in the CDM, the key consideration is cost – either in terms of achieving their emission reduction commitments at the lowest possible cost, or in terms of making profit from trading in CERs. Even the option of concluding forward contracts is often bypassed in favour of the less risky option of buying CERs on the spot market (Capoor and Ambrosi 2008: 32). As highlighted above, even though under forward contracts there is no direct investment provided, some foreign entities will provide upfront payment of part of the purchase price, which can then be used to cover transaction costs and/or leverage finance for the underlying project. However, even this option is being by-passed, making the situation worse for those countries that rely on foreign involvement in projects.

Many countries, especially LDCs and African countries, rely on foreign investment and capacity building to be able to develop and host projects. For example, Pfeifer and Stiles point out that mechanisms for local financing of small-scale projects in Africa are very limited, and that this limits the opportunities to develop unilateral projects (Pfeifer and Stiles 2008, supra note 129, at 17). Sieghart concluded that a key barrier to unilateral CDM projects in LDCs such as Yemen is difficulties in procuring underlying finance and emphasised the need to address this problem in the interest of LDCs (Sieghart 2009: 202). Although there is no doubt that host country entities will benefit from unilateral projects through the associated CER revenues, some countries lack the financial and technical capability to exploit their CDM potential and will thus be unable to enjoy the sustainable development benefits (such as direct investment, capacity building and technology transfer) to which the CDM is meant to contribute.

Consequently, the countries affected by this barrier are those most in need of the benefits of the CDM, because of their low human development, as most lack the technical and financial capacity to unilaterally develop and implement projects. This barrier created by the unilateral CDM structure, therefore, mainly undermines the 'need' factor for achieving equitable distribution. However, as already highlighted several times, because those countries with the greatest need also have emission reduction potential, this barrier also undermines the 'potential' factor.

8.2 The market-based nature of the CDM

Although the CDM was created as a mechanism that would both generate cost-effective emission reductions and contribute to sustainable development, the very nature of the CDM as a market-based instrument is preventing it from achieving these objectives equitably among developing countries. The nature of the CDM means that, apart from the necessary environmental constraints,[6] normal market forces, such as risk and cost, largely dictate the location of projects. Investors are generally more interested in lower-cost and -risk projects, with the cost of a CDM project and the profit to be derived from it being the major considerations. This has resulted in investment directed mainly towards the larger developing countries that can supply these kinds of project. This is despite the fact that, unlike normal foreign direct investment, the CDM is not targeted at enabling investors to make profit from CDM projects. It is a mechanism that has (environmental) objectives of contributing to sustainable development in developing countries and providing cost-effective GHG emission reductions for developed countries.

Added to the problem is the fact that the sustainable development element of the CDM, unlike its GHG emission reduction element, has no monetary value put on it and is, therefore, not factored into the cost or profit of the CDM. According to the CDM rules, the host developing countries are responsible for verifying and confirming that projects will contribute to their sustainable development (Decision 3/CMP.1, Annex, paragraph 40(a)). The host entity also usually provides, in the PDD, an explanation of the sustainable development contributions of the project. In addition, the CDM Executive Board adopted a CDM sustainable development tool in late 2012, which CDM project participants and coordinating/managing entities can use to describe the sustainable development co-benefits of a CDM project activity or PoA.[7]

Beyond these, there are no regulations or rules concerning the value or requirement of sustainable development under the CDM. Other than the confirmation by the host country of the sustainable development contributions of the CDM (which does not need to be proved or backed up by evidence), the other regulations regarding the sustainable development contributions of the CDM are voluntary, and their use adds nothing to the income generated from CDM projects.

6   Such as rules to ensure that projects result in real, measurable and long-term benefits related to the mitigation of climate change, and that reductions in emissions are additional to any that would occur in the absence of the certified project activity. See Protocol Article 12.
7   See: www.research.net/s.aspx?sm=fBHUkNX7wgrEEuYH1VpaoMl7lElJ330Py2S0zwG3Iak%3d#q1

There is, therefore, no market incentive to promote sustainable development and no particular benefit to investors of investing in projects with high sustainable development contributions (Sutter and Parreño 2007: 89; Newell 2012: 3). Because of this, for investors who are considering cost and profit, the GHG reduction element is usually the paramount consideration, as, when calculating profit, investors mainly calculate profit generated from the GHG emission reductions achieved. As a result, countries with the potential for low-cost, low-risk and high-profit projects will be the first choice. It is partly because of this barrier, caused by the market-based nature of CDM projects, that the size of projects (which partly determine the profit to be achieved from projects) and cost-related issues also constitute barriers to equitable distribution.

The consequence of this is that those developing countries that are rapidly industrialising, with the attendant industries, high emission levels, institutions and possibly project experience or existing foreign direct investment, are better placed to host CDM projects, and investors will gravitate towards these countries. This is compounded by the CDM no longer being used purely as a compliance tool by developed country entities, but also as a profit-generating mechanism. This means that, although many public and private entities invest in the CDM in order to use the CERs generated to meet their emission reduction commitments or to comply with environmental regulations in their jurisdictions, many invest in the CDM in order to trade the CERs generated and make profit from such trade.[8] Because of this, these entities would not only go for projects that cost the least, they will, in particular, go for projects that can generate the greatest profit, and most likely follow the normal foreign direct investment trends.

It is worth noting that this relates mainly to bilateral projects in which the developed country entities invest directly in the underlying projects and are, therefore, primarily interested in reducing the cost of investing and generating the biggest profit they can. It also applies to some unilateral projects, however, particularly where the foreign entity purchaser, although not providing financing for the underlying project, agrees, through a forward contract, to purchase the CERs (before these are generated or even before the project is registered). In this case, the purchaser is interested in projects that will generate sufficient quantities of CERs that would make the transaction worth their while.

Although these issues are important to the CDM and to investors and should be considered, the important point is that market-based indicators are only suitable for one element of the CDM – the GHG emission reduction element. Chapter 5 points out that, to achieve equitable distribution,

---

8   See the CDM Pipeline, 1 March 2013, for the list of CDM investors/CER purchasers. Compliance buyers include those identified as 'public' or 'utility', and traders are generally identified as 'carbon market'.

countries' need or sustainable development potential must be considered. Therefore, the sustainable development element of the CDM must be considered, if the CDM is to actually achieve its dual objectives. Unfortunately, market-based indicators do not compute this element. It is not suggested that the CDM should no longer operate as a market, nor have market characteristics. However, it is essential that, to ensure achievement of both objectives of the CDM, while investors consider market factors in selecting host countries and projects, they also consider sustainable development factors, such as countries' need and sustainable development potential. A combination of the two, rather than just the cost-effectiveness factor, should guide investors' choices.

The barrier to equitable distribution presented by the market-based nature of the CDM mainly undermines the 'need' factor for achieving equitable distribution. This is because, by not considering countries' need and sustainable development potential, investors are not adequately considering the specific circumstances of those countries with the greatest need and a high sustainable development potential. If countries' need and sustainable development potential were actually considered by investors, then, it follows that those countries with the greatest need and sustainable development potential would be given some preference over those countries with less need and sustainable development potential, or at least that they would have the opportunity to participate more effectively in the CDM. In addition, because these countries (with the greatest need) also have emission reduction potential, their inadequate participation in the CDM due to this market barrier also undermines the 'potential' factor for achieving equitable distribution.

8.3 Conclusion

The two barriers identified in this chapter – the prevalence of unilateral projects and the CDM's market structure – are fundamental barriers to equitable distribution, and both combine to put those countries most in need at a severe disadvantage in terms of project hosting.

For example, take a developed country entity that requires an extra 100,000 CO_2e to contribute towards meeting its compliance target and decides to obtain 100,000 CERs from the CDM for this purpose. This entity has the option of purchasing the CERs from a unilateral project or investing in a project and using the CERs generated to meet its target, or a mixture of both. If the entity decides to use CERs generated from a unilateral project, odds are that it would purchase the CERs from a larger developing country, because, as shown, such a country would be in the best position to offer unilaterally generated CERs.

If, however, the entity decides to invest directly in a CDM project (rather than simply purchase CERs) and use the CERs generated to meet its target, again, chances are that it would choose one of the larger, rapidly industrialising developing countries in which to invest. This is because, owing to the market nature of the CDM, in which risk and cost are key and sustainable development benefits are not quantified, such countries would be more attractive because of their greater capacity to host projects, greater potential for larger projects (and, therefore, better economies of scale), probably more favourable and better-developed investment climate, and less risk. Either way, the smaller developing countries are at a disadvantage. Michaelowa points out that sub-Saharan African countries are at a double disadvantage because they would be unable to attract foreign investors for bilateral or multilateral projects owing to perceived country risk, and they would also be unable to carry out unilateral projects owing, for example, to lack of human capacity and availability of domestic capital (Michaelowa 2007: 28). The UNFCCC Secretariat states that:

> As many CDM project activities are domestically financed, a lack of access to early stage seed funding for CDM costs and high unit trans-action costs are significant barriers in many poorer countries. The lack of underlying project finance prevents CDM projects from moving ahead in underrepresented countries.
>
> (UNFCCC 2012: 9)

Most of the barriers to equitable distribution identified in Chapter 7 actually constitute barriers because of these two fundamental barriers. For example, lack of capacity and lack of access to financing are barriers because, as the CDM currently operates, most countries develop and implement projects themselves, with no or limited foreign involvement. They, therefore, require sufficient capacity, together with access to sufficient local financing, to cover the transaction and implementation costs.

The Chapter 7 barriers themselves are not created by these two funda-mental barriers: countries lack capacity and adequate access to financing because of their low development levels, not because of the market structure of the CDM. However, lack of capacity and lack of access to financing constitute barriers to CDM participation because, rather than the CDM operating bilaterally as originally envisaged, the CDM market is dominated by unilateral projects. For instance, lack of access to financing for project transaction and implementation costs would be less of a barrier if, as originally intended, developed country entities actually invested directly in projects, rather than simply buying the CERs they generate.

The overall conclusion, therefore, is that the fundamental barriers to equitable distribution of CDM projects are: the market-based nature of the CDM market, in which cost-effectiveness, risk minimisation and profit maximisation are key, and the sustainable development contributions of CDM projects are not monetised; and the dominance of unilateral CDM projects in the CDM market, the potential for which those countries with the greatest need do not have or are unable to access. Until and unless these two fundamental barriers, which also affect how the CDM operates, are addressed, the CDM will not be able to achieve equity in the distribution of projects.

To address the barriers to equitable distribution, various mechanisms have been created under the CDM. These mechanisms are the focus of the next chapter, which analyses these mechanisms and their impact on the distribution of projects.

9 Measures for promoting equitable distribution

Countries have long recognised the need to make a special effort to ensure a more equitable distribution of projects under the CDM. Without actions specifically aimed at promoting equitable distribution, the CDM will remain tipped in favour of just a few countries, and most countries will enjoy only limited participation in the mechanism. That is why, under the CDM regime, many measures have been taken for this purpose. This chapter focuses on these measures and examines them in the context of the barriers to equitable distribution identified in Chapters 7 and 8.

As outlined in Chapters 7 and 8, the barriers to equitable distribution of projects are lack of technical and financial capacity, preference for large-scale projects, prevalence of unilateral projects and the market nature of the CDM. Although little effort has gone into addressing some of these barriers, for others, such as lack of technical and financial capacity, attempts are being made to address them within the regime through various initiatives such as payment exemptions (to address cost-related barriers) and capacity-building initiatives, such as the Nairobi Framework. This chapter examines some of these measures, with the specific aim of ascertaining whether enough is being done under the CDM regime to address the problem of inequitable distribution of projects.

In addition, it uses the two factors of equitable distribution identified in Chapter 5 – need and potential – and assesses whether the various mechanisms adequately take these into consideration in their design or operation. As discussed in Chapter 5, in order to achieve an equitable distribution of projects, countries' need and potential must be fully taken into consideration, and countries with the greatest need (identified in Chapter 6), must be given preferential treatment to support their participation in the CDM. Therefore, when examining the mechanisms for promoting equitable distribution, this chapter also considers whether the mechanisms adequately consider countries' need and potential, as well as whether the countries with the greatest need receive adequate preferential treatment from the mechanisms.

9.1 Addressing the capacity barrier

The CDM is an innovative mechanism, and, when it was established, most countries had no idea how to access the benefits it promised. As a result, many capacity-building initiatives were launched to help build countries' capacity, although it was acknowledged that a lot of lessons would have to be 'learned by doing'. However, even now, almost 10 years and 6,000 plus projects later, lack of capacity is still a problem for many countries. That is why, in addition to the many general capacity-building initiatives undertaken in its early days, the CDM regime is also undertaking several initiatives aimed primarily at those countries that still lack capacity to effectively participate in the CDM. It is on this latter group of initiatives that this section focuses.

One of the main capacity-building mechanisms under the CDM regime is the *Nairobi Framework*. This initiative was launched at COP/MOP 2 in November 2006, with the aim of helping all developing countries, especially those in sub-Saharan Africa, to improve their participation in the CDM. The framework was first announced by the UN Secretary-General during his address at the Conference (Decision 1/CMP.2) (UN 2006). It was initiated by five agencies – the UNFCCC Secretariat, the UNEP, the UNDP, the African Development Bank and the World Bank. The United Nations Conference on Trade and Development and the United Nations Institute for Training and Research subsequently joined the initiative, bringing the total number of Nairobi Framework partner agencies to seven.

The aim of the framework is, among other things, to 'catalyse the CDM in Africa'[1] and it has five objectives, all aimed at enhancing different aspects of CDM capacity. The objectives of the Nairobi Framework are to: build and enhance DNA capacity; build capacity to develop CDM projects; promote investment opportunities for projects; improve information sharing, outreach and exchange of views on activities, as well as education and training; and enhance inter-agency coordination.[2] The UNFCCC Secretariat has also identified some of the possible elements of each of these objectives, based on the needs to be addressed by the framework, and also identified some of the activities that could be undertaken to achieve the objectives.[3] In recognition of their limited CDM capacity and to help increase their participation in the CDM, the framework aims to build the capacity of

---

1 See the Nairobi Framework webpage, 'Regional Distribution – Nairobi Framework' at: http://cdm.unfccc.int/Nairobi_Framework/index.html (UNFCCC, 30 April 2013).
2 Ibid.
3 See 'Elements of the Nairobi Framework' at: http://cdm.unfccc.int/Nairobi_Framework/ Nai_framework_possible_elements.pdf (UNFCCC, 30 April 2013).

African countries to identify, develop, submit and process CDM projects.[4] This essentially means building their capacity to go through the CDM project cycle.

The framework operates through each partner agency, either individually or in partnership with others, undertaking activities in support of the framework. Since the launch of the framework, the partner agencies have carried out a variety of capacity-building and other activities and initiatives.[5]

An example of such activities is the *Africa Carbon Forum*. The first Africa Carbon Forum was held in September 2008 and aimed to strengthen links between CDM project developers and the African region's investment community, as well as to provide opportunities for DNAs to exchange views and share experiences on the CDM. It was organised by the partner agencies in collaboration with the International Emissions Trading Association and combined a carbon investment trade fair with targeted CDM capacity building.[6] There have now been four such events, and the fifth was scheduled for July 2013, on the theme 'promoting access to low-carbon development in Africa'.[7]

One of the recent initiatives under the framework is the *Regional Collaboration Centres* partnership between the UNFCCC Secretariat and several regional development banks and other institutions. The aim of the partnership is to establish regional collaboration centres to build the CDM capacity of underperforming regions by supporting project identification, providing project design assistance, addressing issues identified by validators, and offering opportunities to reduce transaction costs.[8] The first two regional collaboration centres were established in October 2012 and February 2013 in Lomé, Togo, and Kampala, Uganda, respectively. The partnership aims to establish more centres in Asia, Latin America and the Caribbean.

The *DNA Forum* and *DNA Help Desk* are two capacity-building initiatives under the CDM regime. The DNA Forum was established by the CDM Executive Board in response to the request by COP/MOP 1 for the

---

4 See the Concept Note for the Nairobi Framework Mobilization Event held at the twenty-sixth meeting of the UNFCCC Subsidiary Bodies, in May 2006 at: http://cdm.unfccc.int/ Nairobi_Framework/Nai_framework_mobSB26.pdf (UNFCCC, 30 April 2013).
5 For a report of the framework's 2012 activities, see 'Nairobi Framework Partnership 2012 Annual Report' online. Available at: http://cdm.unfccc.int/Nairobi_Framework/NFP_2012_anrep.pdf (accessed 30 April 2013). For the framework's 2013 work plan, see 'Nairobi Framework Partnership Workplan 2013' online. Available at: http://cdm.unfccc. int/Nairobi_Framework/NFP_wp_2013.pdf (accessed 30 April 2013).
6 See Akanle T. *et al.* (2008).
7 See the 2013 Forum website online. Available at: http://africacarbonforum.com/2013/ english/index.htm (accessed 30 April 2013).
8 See the regional collaboration centres website. Online. Available at: http://cdm.unfccc.int/ stakeholder/rcc/index.html (accessed 30 April 2013).

organisation of DNA Forum meetings to help broaden participation in the CDM (Decision 7/CMP.1, paragraph 36). The forum is held regularly and aims to provide an information exchange platform, enabling DNAs to share their experiences regarding the CDM, and also provide an opportunity for DNAs to bring common views and issues to the attention of the Executive Board.[9] The DNA Forum is, therefore, specifically targeted at enhancing DNA capacity by providing a platform for DNAs to interact with one another and exchange information, experiences, problems and best practices in relation to the CDM process.

The DNA Help Desk provides advice and support to DNAs from LDCs, SIDS, Africa and countries that had fewer than ten registered projects as of 31 December 2012. DNAs from these countries can request advice and support from the help desk on a variety of issues, such as the submission of proposals for standardised baselines.[10]

Another capacity-building initiative under the CDM regime is the *CDM Bazaar*. The CDM Executive Board, during its twenty-first meeting, identified as one of its functions the development of a publicly available database of CDM project activities.[11] To implement this, the CDM Bazaar was launched by the UNFCCC Secretariat and the UNEP Risoe Centre to facilitate the exchange of information about CDM projects and opportunities, with the ultimate aim of 'creating an efficient global CDM market'.[12] The CDM Bazaar was not specifically established as an equitable distribution initiative. Rather it is essentially a capacity-building and information-sharing tool for all CDM participants, particularly developing country participants.

The bazaar is a web-based, free information platform, which provides information on CDM buyers, sellers and service providers. It is designed to provide information about CDM opportunities and lists specific CDM projects and CDM project ideas, notices about CERs for sale, as well as the profiles of CDM market participants, such as investors, buyers and sellers. Potential host countries can thus 'advertise' project ideas and potential projects that they would like to see developed in their countries as CDM projects. Examples include project ideas for a green loan credit line in Tajikistan[13] and for a fossil fuel switch project in Uganda.[14]

---

9 See the DNA Forum webpage online. Available at: http://cdm.unfccc.int/DNA/DNAForum/index.html (accessed 30 April 2013).

10 See 'DNA Help Desk'. Online. Available at: http://cdm.unfccc.int/DNA/helpdesk (accessed 30 April 2013).

11 See 'CDM Management Plan' Annex 25 of the Report of the 21st Meeting of the Executive Board (18 October 2005). Online. Available at: http://cdm.unfccc.int/EB/021/eb21repan25.pdf, 17 (accessed 30 April 2013).

12 See the CDM Bazaar website. Online. Available at: www.cdmbazaar.net/about (accessed 30 April 2013).

As an information-sharing tool, it aims to make relevant CDM information readily and easily available to interested stakeholders in the process, thus facilitating their participation. It is in this sense that it aims to contribute to the equitable distribution of projects, by helping facilitate the participation of countries in the CDM, through the provision of relevant information.

The Nairobi Framework and the other capacity-building initiatives discussed above all aim to build the capacity of developing countries to participate in the CDM. As highlighted in Chapter 7, lack of capacity and local expertise is one of the barriers to equitable distribution of CDM projects, and it particularly affects those countries with the lowest human development and greatest need, as they generally have the least capacity and experience. These initiatives are a start to addressing this barrier and to ensuring equitable distribution of CDM projects.

It is, however, difficult to assess the effectiveness of these capacity mechanisms, specifically because of the difficulty of linking specific capacity-building activities to any improvements in countries' participation in the CDM. Nonetheless, it is clear that, for example, as a group, LDCs and African countries are still significantly underperforming compared with other countries, despite the number of capacity-building mechanisms that target these countries, such as the various initiatives under the Nairobi Framework. Although the number of projects hosted by African countries has increased from 11 (in December 2006) to 48 (in November 2010) to 136 (March 2013), the region's share has not improved, changing from 2.61 per cent (December 2006) to 1.9 per cent (November 2010) to 2 per cent (in March 2013).[15]

With regard to the DNA Forum and the DNA Help Desk, it can only be noted that, as insufficient DNA capacity is one of the barriers to equitable distribution, initiatives such as these have the potential to help address the problem. Nevertheless, because lack of DNA capacity remains a problem, there is a need for continued capacity building for the DNAs of the countries with the greatest need. Such capacity building should directly address the capacity needs of DNAs and help them to be more effective in carrying out their functions. The DNA Forum can be used to identify what tools or skills DNAs are lacking (such as the ability to identify and promote CDM projects), and they should then be supported to acquire these skills.

13 See 'CDM Project Idea: Green Loan Credit Line.' Online. Available at: www.cdmbazaar. net/repo/project_ideas/project_idea-165283668.0 (accessed 30 April 2013).
14 See 'CDM Project Idea: Sameer's Environment Conservation Project through Boiler Fuel Switch to Biomass.' Online. Available at: www.cdmbazaar.net/repo/project_ideas/project_ idea-297196027.0 (accessed 30 April 2013).
15 CDM Pipeline, 1 March 2013. Online. Available at: http://cdmpipeline.org/ (accessed 10 April 2013).

Chapter 11 contains a more detailed discussion of other ways of addressing this capacity barrier.

The CDM Bazaar also aims to help facilitate countries' participation in the CDM by providing a platform to share information regarding, among other things, project ideas and proposed projects. Again, the success of this initiative is not easy to evaluate, but, whereas some of the project ideas advertised on the Bazaar may have been developed and registered as CDM projects, many of them, such as those by Zimbabwe and Uganda, have not been registered.[16] This suggests that the CDM Bazaar has not been completely successful in achieving its objectives. Also, as of April 2013, there were only forty-four projects listed in the database, and only one of these was added in 2013. Considering that there are over 6,500 registered projects and another 2,500 in the pipeline, the CDM Bazaar is obviously not being adequately utilised.

As discussed in Chapter 5, in order to achieve equitable distribution, there is a need for preferential treatment to be given to the countries that have the greatest need. These countries should receive support to enable their effective participation in the CDM, provided they have sufficient emission reduction potential to make the preferential treatment, such as targeted capacity building, worthwhile. And, as shown in Chapter 6, many of the countries with the greatest need also have emission reduction potential, and there is therefore no real reason why they should not be performing better under the CDM.

Some of the capacity-building mechanisms examined above, such as the Africa Carbon Forum and the DNA Help Desk, appear to be providing this preferential treatment by targeting some of the countries with the greatest need, such as African countries and LDCs. Nevertheless, much more is required. Given that lack of capacity is still a major barrier to equitable distribution, particularly for those countries with the greatest need, more targeted capacity building is required, designed specifically to address the capacity problems of these countries.

9.2 Addressing the transaction costs barrier

With regard to the transaction costs associated with investing in certain groups of countries, some steps have been taken to help to reduce these costs. First, in order to support a more equitable regional distribution of projects by reducing the transaction costs associated with CDM projects in LDCs and thus making these projects more attractive, the share-of-proceeds levy and registration fee for CDM projects were abolished for projects hosted in

16 For details of these project ideas, see 'CDM Project Ideas'. Online. Available at: www.cdmbazaar.net/overview?listing_type=project_idea (accessed 30 April 2013).

LDCs (Decision 17/CP.7, paragraph 15(b); Decision 2/CMP.3, paragraph 31). This means that, for CDM projects hosted by LDCs, there is no registration fee to pay, and also no amount will be deducted upon issuance of CERs to cover the share-of-proceeds levy for administration expenses and adaptation.

Second, for countries with fewer than ten registered project activities, the payment of the registration fee has been deferred until after the first issuance of CERs (Decision 2/CMP.5, paragraph 47). This deferment means that these countries do not have to source financing to cover this registration fee, but can cover the payment after the first issuance of CERs, presumably from the revenue generated from the sale of the CERs.

In addition, the CDM Loan Scheme was launched in April 2012 to provide interest-free loans to countries with fewer than ten registered projects, to help these countries pay certain project transaction costs: the costs of developing PDDs, and of the validation and first verification of projects. These loans will be provided from the interest accrued on the principal of the CDM Trust Fund, as well as any voluntary contributions from donors, and will be repaid starting from the first issuance of CERs (Decision 2/CMP.5, paragraphs 49–50; Decision 3/CMP.6, Annex III). The scheme is run jointly by the UNFCCC Secretariat, the UNEP Risoe Centre and the United Nations Office for Project Services.[17]

The approach of these initiatives is to make investing in projects hosted by a specific group of countries more financially attractive than they would otherwise be, by reducing some of the transaction costs associated with the projects. In the case of the loan scheme, the aim is to make accessing funds, albeit for the project transaction costs, easier for project developers.

As already highlighted several times, in order to ensure an equitable distribution of projects, preferential treatment should be given to those countries with the greatest need, in order to help them increase their participation in the CDM. LDCs fall in this category, as they are among the countries with the greatest need/lowest human development.[18] Therefore, by exempting projects hosted in LDCs from payment of transaction costs, the CDM has taken a step towards ensuring a more equitable distribution of projects. In addition, because many LDCs do have some emission reduction potential (some have high potential and some medium, although there are those with low potential), this initiative also goes some way in meeting the 'potential' factor for achieving equitable distribution, because, as shown in Chapter 6, most LDCs are significantly underperforming in the CDM and are not fulfilling their potential. This payment exemption initiative, therefore, ticks all the boxes regarding the factors for achieving

17 See the CDM Loan Scheme website. Online. Available at: www.cdmloanscheme.org/ (accessed 30 April 2013).
18 See the discussion and classification in Chapter 4.

equitable distribution – it provides preferential treatment to those countries with the greatest need that also have emission reduction potential.

However, although this initiative is undoubtedly a good one, it does not appear to have been particularly successful in helping LDCs effectively and equitably participate in the CDM. The payment exemption was introduced in 2001, before the first CDM project was registered.[19] As of March 2013, out of the forty-nine LDCs, only sixteen of them host projects – all sixteen host a total of fifty-seven projects between them. That is 57 out of a total of 6,556 registered projects – less than 1 per cent. As the analysis in Chapter 6 shows, LDCs are not currently fulfilling their CDM potential in terms of GHG emission reduction potential, and so the reason for this poor performance cannot be said to be a lack of emission reduction potential in these countries. And, from the fact that this initiative has not been completely successful, it is obvious that there are issues other than transaction costs that influence CDM project hosting. Therefore, although this initiative may have contributed to these countries being able to participate in the CDM, more obviously needs to be done to ensure that CDM projects are more equitably distributed among all developing countries, including LDCs.

The loans that will be made available to countries currently hosting fewer than ten registered projects will undoubtedly be helpful to these countries, and, combined with the deferment of the payment of the registration fee, will contribute to overcoming the transaction cost barrier in these countries. As high transaction costs constitute a barrier partly because they are incurred up front (before the project begins to generate income), these initiatives will help countries that cannot raise sufficient upfront financing. Nonetheless, only time will tell how successful the initiative will be in helping these countries increase their participation in the CDM, because, as noted above, the similar initiative for LDCs has not been particularly successful in promoting the participation of LDCs.

However, the loans scheme is not in accordance with the factors for achieving equitable distribution identified in Chapter 3 (that is, need, potential and preferential treatment for those with the greatest need). This is because the payment postponement and the loans are to be made available to all countries with fewer than ten registered projects, regardless of their GHG emission reduction potential or their need. It is also not restricted to countries with the greatest need, which is what is advocated in Chapter 6. Consequently, countries such as Barbados, Singapore and Qatar, which have low need, will be as eligible to receive these loans as countries such as the Democratic Republic of the Congo and Zambia, which have very high need. It also means that countries such as Antigua and Barbuda and Saint Lucia, which have very low emission reduction potential, will also be as eligible to

---

19 Decision 17/CP.7, which establishes the exemption, was adopted by the parties in COP 7 in 2001. The first CDM project entered the CDM pipeline in December 2003.

receive these loans as countries such as Myanmar and Nigeria, which have high emission reduction potential. Such generic preferential treatment, therefore, does not adequately consider the specific circumstances of countries and would not be an effective use of resources, as resources would be better targeted at those countries that need them the most, particularly those that also have sufficient GHG emission reduction potential. In this regard, this preferential treatment (given to all countries with fewer than ten registered projects) falls short of the effort needed to achieve equitable distribution.

9.3 Addressing the size of projects barrier

In order to overcome the size barrier to equitable distribution of projects, two initiatives have been adopted within the CDM framework, specifically to reduce the transaction costs of small-scale projects, therefore making them more financially attractive. First, projects expected to achieve fewer than 15,000 tonnes of CO_2e emission reductions annually (that is, expected to generate fewer than 15,000 CERs) have been exempted from paying the project registration fee (Report of the 37th Meeting of the CDM Executive Board, Annex 20, paragraph 4). This is similar to the registration fee exemption granted to projects hosted in LDCs.

In addition, and in recognition of the fact that the costs associated with developing small-scale CDM projects may exceed the financial benefits achievable from such projects because of their size, the COP/MOP at its second session adopted simplified modalities for small-scale CDM projects, the aim of which is to reduce the transaction costs associated with this type of project. The simplified modalities and procedures include: a simplified PDD; simplified methodologies for baseline and monitoring plans; simplified provisions for environmental impact analysis; lower project registration fee; a shorter review period for the registration of projects; and permitting the same designated operational entity to validate, as well as verify and certify, emission reductions for specific projects (Decision 4/CMP.1, Annex II).

A third measure under the CDM regime that aims to make smaller projects more attractive is the CDM PoA. This programmatic approach under the CDM was introduced in 2005 to reduce the transaction costs of small projects (or projects that would produce relatively few emission reductions) and thereby make these more attractive to investors (UNEP 2009: 9). The CDM PoA works by allowing an unlimited number of similar project activities to be registered under a single programme. Once a PoA undergoes the project cycle and is registered, an unlimited number of CPAs can then be added to this programme over time, without them having to undergo the entire registration process, provided they meet the eligibility criteria.[20]

20 See 'Programme of Activities'. Online. Available at: http://cdm.unfccc.int/ProgrammeOf Activities/index.html (accessed 5 April 2013). The requirements are outlined in the Clean

The obvious advantage of this is that it reduces the transaction costs associated with undergoing the project cycle. For example, no registration fee is due for each CPA included after registration. The second advantage is that small project activities that would not be viable as stand-alone CDM projects, because their transaction costs would be too high or the CERs they would generate would be too low, can be included under a PoA. This also means that, theoretically, a PoA can generate an unlimited volume of emission reductions/CERs, as an unlimited number of CPAs can be added to a PoA. The PoA, therefore, makes small- or micro-scale projects more financially attractive, and makes the CDM more accessible to countries, such as LDCs, that have a greater potential for such projects.

An example of a CDM PoA is the Uganda Municipal Waste Compost Programme, registered in April 2010. Under this PoA, organic matter from municipal solid waste is recovered as compost in order to avoid the methane emissions that would otherwise have resulted from the use of landfills. At the time of registration, the intention was to include multiple towns and cities under the programme (each activity would likely have been too small for the CDM, but bringing several of such activities under a PoA made them more financially viable). As of April 2013, there were a total of nine CPAs under this PoA in nine different municipalities – the first was included at the point of PoA registration in April 2010, seven were included in April 2011, and the ninth was included in December 2012.[21]

As with the exemption from payment of the registration fee, the aim of these measures is to reduce the transaction costs associated with small-scale projects, in order to make them more financially attractive than they would otherwise be. If both large- and small-scale projects bore the same transaction costs, this would be disadvantageous to small-scale projects, as a larger percentage (proportionately) of the proceeds of the project would go towards these costs, than for large-scale projects. These simplified modalities and resulting lower transaction costs, together with the registration fee payment exemption, would be particularly beneficial to smaller, less industrialised developing countries, which do not have large industries suitable for large-scale CDM projects, or only have a few of such opportunities, and therefore greater potential for small-scale projects. These measures would, in theory, improve their chances of attracting CDM investment.

Regarding how effective these initiatives have been in addressing the problem of equitable distribution, although undoubtedly well intentioned

Development Mechanism Project Standard, which can be accessed online. Available at: http://cdm.unfccc.int/Reference/Standards/index.html (accessed 25 June 2013).

21 For all the details of this PoA, see 'PoA 2956: Uganda Municipal Waste Compost Programme.' Online. Available at: http://cdm.unfccc.int/ProgrammeOfActivities/poa_db/ JL4B8R2DKF90NE6YXCVOQ3MWSGT5UA/view (accessed 30 April 2013). The list of CPAs can be seen online. Available at: http://cdm.unfccc.int/ProgrammeOfActivities/poa_ db/JL4B8R2DKF90NE6YXCVOQ3MWSGT5UA/viewCPAs (accessed 30 April 2013).

and of benefit to some countries, they have not actually achieved this goal. Even if the measure has contributed to making small-scale projects more financially attractive and resulted in an increase in the number of projects that would otherwise have been implemented, it has not helped achieve a more equitable distribution of projects. Although, as of April 2013, small-scale projects made up about 38 per cent of the CDM pipeline, the distribution of these projects is nearly identical to the distribution of CDM projects generally. For example, out of the 2,494 registered small-scale projects, 828 and 747 are in India and China, respectively, but only a total of 33 in the forty-nine LDCs and 47 in the entire African region (CDM Pipeline, 1 March 2013). It does not appear, therefore, that this initiative has been particularly beneficial to those categories requiring special attention under the CDM (those with the greatest need, such as the LDCs and others identified in Chapter 5), but has rather benefited those that already had an advantage within the CDM process.

The reason for this is partly because these measures are not in accordance with the factors for achieving equitable distribution. The three measures are available to all developing countries, irrespective of their need and emission reduction potential – they do not give preferential treatment to the countries with the greatest need. All countries can take advantage of the measures, meaning those that were already at a disadvantage remain so – these measures do not give them any greater advantage.

In the case of the PoA, this measure is still in its early days, with only 134 registered as of April 2013. It is, therefore, too early to judge how successful it will be in increasing the participation of underperforming countries, particularly those with the greatest need. However, the current distribution shows that certain groups of countries are doing better under the PoA than under the CDM itself, even though the distribution is not completely even. For instance, LDCs currently host 8 per cent of registered PoAs (11 out of the 134 registered), compared with the 0.86 per cent of registered CDM projects. Although it is still a small number, as it is still relatively early days, there is hope that this number will increase over time and enable LDCs and other countries in need to access the benefits of the CDM.

9.4 Barriers not being addressed under the CDM regime

As highlighted at the start of this chapter, although the CDM regime has instituted some measures to address some of the barriers to equitable distribution, there are still several barriers that are not being addressed under the regime. These barriers are the lack of finance for the underlying project, the prevalence of unilateral projects in the CDM market and the market nature of the CDM itself. There are currently no measures or initiatives within the CDM framework to address these barriers.

Regarding the finance for implementing projects, the various financing initiatives aim to reduce transaction costs, but do not directly assist with implementation costs. However, implementation costs comprise the bulk of the financing required for CDM projects. In addition, as already noted, most developed country participants in the CDM market do not provide finance for the underlying projects – local developers must source this finance themselves. Sieghart, for example, notes that project developers do not perceive transaction costs as the major financial barrier, but that developers face difficulties in securing underlying finance (Sieghart 2009: 201). Those countries that are the most affected by this barrier are the countries that, in fact, have the greatest need – the LDCs and many African countries.[22] In this respect, therefore, the CDM regime fails to consider the need of these countries in efforts to promote a more equitable distribution of projects.

There are also no measures to address the prevalence of unilateral CDM projects. For instance, there is no limit to the percentage of unilateral projects in the CDM pipeline, nor any kind of requirement for a minimum share or percentage of bilateral projects. As only those developing countries that have the financial and technical capacity to identify, develop and implement projects can effectively implement unilateral projects, many of the poorer developing nations are excluded from effectively participating in the CDM.

The CDM regime also provides no measures to address the problems created by its market nature. The responsibility to ascertain that CDM projects contribute to countries' sustainable development belongs to host countries themselves (Decision 3/CMP.1, Annex, paragraph 40(a)). Developed country entities are not required to consider the sustainable development contribution of projects or potential of countries when investing in projects. There is no added benefit to them (except perhaps goodwill or public policy) of investing in projects with particularly high sustainable development contributions or in countries with high sustainable development potential (Halvorssen 2005: 367). There are no real incentives for investors or CER purchasers acting in the CDM market, other than cost or profit.

There are, however, some voluntary schemes that have developed a premium for projects with high sustainable development benefits. An example of such schemes is the Gold Standard, which has the aim of ensuring that CDM projects foster sustainable development in developing countries, in addition to producing cost-effective emission reductions.[23] Another example involves efforts by the European Union to develop its own sustainability criteria. For instance, credits from large-scale hydro and forestry projects, among others, are banned from inclusion in the European Union Emission Trading Scheme (EU ETS), on the grounds of ensuring the environmental integrity of the CDM (van Asselt 2009).[24]

22 See Chapter 4 for a classification of countries according to their need.
23 See *The Gold Standard Brochure 2012*. Online. Available at: www.cdmgoldstandard.org/wp-content/uploads/2011/09/GS-brochure-2012-Final-web.pdf (accessed 24 June 2013).

Precisely because the CDM is a market, there may be concerns about the level of regulation that can be imposed on the market, including on actors in the market.[25] In particular, there may be questions about whether the CDM legal regime can impose restrictions on, for example, which countries investors should invest in, or compel or require them to invest in certain countries. However, the fact is that the CDM *is* a regulated market, and there are already restrictions on the countries (only countries that fulfil the eligibility criteria) and kinds of project investors can invest in (Decision 17/CP.7, Preamble, paragraph 5; Decision 17/CP.7, paragraph 7(a)). Some of these rules, such as the additionality requirement, were established to ensure the environmental integrity of the CDM and ensure it actually fulfils its objective of real GHG emission reductions (Curnow and Hodes 2009: 33).

In the same manner, it should be possible to regulate the CDM market to enable the CDM to meets its objective of contributing to sustainable development in developing countries, and not limiting this to just some developing countries. There is no real reason why this cannot be done, especially for compliance investors, where the ultimate aim is to ensure that they are able to meet their Kyoto commitments in a more cost-effective way than they can in their own jurisdictions, and not necessarily to make profit.

Owing, therefore, to its current structure, although the CDM may stimulate sustainable development in some developing countries, some countries will still be left behind, because of their inability to compete with the larger industrialising developing countries in terms of the capacity and expertise to develop and implement projects, as well as the availability of local financing and/or the ability to raise the financing for the underlying project.

9.5 Conclusion

The various efforts to address the lack of equitable distribution, such as efforts to reduce the transaction costs of smaller projects or introduce simplified modalities for such projects and the various capacity-building initiatives, have not resulted in a more equitable distribution. This is primarily because these barriers are merely symptomatic of the real problem – the basic design of the CDM regime. Slightly lower transactions costs will not result in projects in smaller developing countries being as attractive as those in larger developing countries, as long as the only considerations

24 See 'A view on CDM qualitative restrictions'. Online. Available at: http://ec.europa.eu/clima/consultations/0004/registered/enel_3_en.pdf (Europa, 21 April 2011).
25 For example, during the negotiations at COP/MOP 5 in December 2009 (at which the author was in attendance), some countries objected to the idea of establishing country quotas, questioning the suitability of such a solution for a market-based instrument.

remain market indicators. Likewise, as long as investors continue to have the option of simply buying CERs rather than investing in CDM projects, particularly as there is no added benefit or incentive to provide direct investment, larger developing countries with the necessary financial and technical capacity will continue to dominate the CDM market.

Unless and until these two issues are addressed, the chances of achieving a truly equitable distribution of CDM projects are very slim. It is, therefore, very important, not only for the CDM to address these problems, but also for countries to take these lessons into consideration when designing a new market mechanism. The next chapter focuses on these two points: it makes recommendations for improving the distribution of projects, and identifies lessons learned for the design of a new market mechanism.

10 Lessons for a new market mechanism and recommendations

With the commencement of the second commitment period of the Kyoto Protocol on 1 January 2013, the CDM is now in its second phase of operation. This second commitment period ends in 2020, coinciding with the expected entry into force of a new global agreement (Decision 1/CMP.8, paragraph 4; Decision 2/CP.18, paragraph 4). It is expected that, at this point, the Kyoto Protocol will come to a natural end. It is unclear what will happen to the CDM at this point, but some of the Kyoto Protocol institutions and mechanisms, including the CDM, might be modified and transferred to this new agreement, to facilitate ease of implementation. Nevertheless, pending this time, the CDM will continue to operate.

In addition, at COP 17 in 2011, countries 'defined' a new market-based mechanism for achieving climate change mitigation, operating under the guidance and authority of the Conference of the Parties (Decision 2/CP.17, paragraph 83). This new mechanism is expected to come into operation as soon as possible (Decision 1/CP.18, paragraph 51(l)), and developed countries will already be able to use units generated by this mechanism to meet their second commitment period targets (Decision 1/CMP.8, Annex I, paragraph J). In much the same way as was done for the CDM, the Subsidiary Body for Scientific and Technological Advice (SBSTA) is now working on the modalities and procedures for this new mechanism, with the aim of recommending a draft decision for adoption by COP 19 in November 2013 (Decision 1/CP.18, paragraph 50).

However, although the modalities for the new mechanism are still unknown, countries did provide some guidance to the SBSTA regarding the possible elements of the new mechanism, including in relation to ensuring a net decrease and/or avoidance of GHG emissions, promoting sustainable development and facilitating the effective participation of private and public entities (Decision 1/CP.18, paragraph 51). It is interesting to note that, despite all the calls for equitable distribution of CDM projects and efforts to promote this, countries did not include ensuring equitable distribution as one of the possible elements of the new mechanism.

As negotiations are still in their very early stages, the outcome with regards to equitable distribution remains to be seen. However, if there are no safeguards in the mechanism to promote equitable distribution, then countries will have missed a great opportunity to learn from the lessons of the CDM and ensure that the new mechanism does not repeat the mistakes of the CDM. One possible reason for countries' reluctance to address this issue at the outset might be their unwillingness to regulate the market.

It is, therefore, useful to consider at this stage whether there is any wisdom in imposing regulations on the CDM and the new market mechanism, considering that they both operate in a market. The fact is that the CDM *is* a regulated market, with regulations prescribing the countries that can participate in the CDM and the types of project that can be registered, and the new mechanism will likewise be operating in a regulated market. Although there is a fear that overregulating the market might drive out investors, the fact is that, under the CDM, developed countries and their entities have been enjoying the benefit of reduced mitigation costs and expect to do the same under the new market mechanism.

The UNFCCC Secretariat reports that, between 2008 and 2012, the CDM is estimated to have saved Annex I countries (both governments and installations/firms in these countries) a total of about US$3.6 billion in compliance costs – savings of US$2.3 billion by firms and US$1.3 billion by governments. This is an estimated total savings of at least US$3.6 billion generated through the use of the CDM in the first commitment period, 2008–12 (UNFCCC 2012: 9, 55–9). The savings are actually expected to be much higher (indirectly), because of the impact of CERs in lowering the price of EU Allowances (UNFCCC 2012: 58–9). Although further regulating the CDM market might result in a reduction in these substantial cost savings, provided that Annex I countries are still able to achieve cost-effective reductions, this should be an acceptable outcome, seeing as the goal is to ensure that the CDM is actually accomplishing both of its goals in an equitable manner. Therefore, there is no valid reason not to put regulations in place to promote a more equitable distribution of projects, but there is everything to aim for.

This is the focus of this chapter. It makes recommendations regarding improvements that can be made to the CDM to ensure that, in its continued operation, it achieves a more equitable distribution of projects than it has so far. In addition, these recommendations should also be taken into consideration in the design of the new market mechanism, in order to ensure that it does not repeat the mistakes of the CDM, and, a few years down the line in its operation, countries are not lamenting the lack of equitable distribution of projects.

Chapter 6 concluded that the current distribution of projects is inequitable because it is not compatible with the definition of equitable distribution provided in Chapter 5, and cannot be explained by countries' GHG emission reduction potential or their need. Thereafter, Chapters 7 and 8 identified the barriers to equitable distribution of CDM projects, as follows: lack of capacity and local expertise; lack of finance for project transaction and implementation costs; size of projects; the prevalence of unilateral CDM projects in the CDM market; and the market-based nature of the CDM. Chapter 8 further highlighted that the two main barriers are the market-based nature of the CDM regime and the prevalence of unilateral CDM projects in the CDM market. As discussed in Chapter 9, some of these barriers are being addressed by the CDM regime. However, there are currently no initiatives within the CDM regime to address these two key barriers.

This chapter addresses what can be done within the CDM regime to remove the barriers to equitable distribution and contribute to a more equitable distribution of CDM projects. These recommendations should also serve as lessons learned for the new market mechanism and any other market mechanisms established in the climate change regime.

10.1 Building countries' capacity

To address the barrier of lack of capacity, as identified in Chapter 7, there is first a need for a comprehensive study to determine countries' capacity, to enable, inter alia, targeted and effective capacity building to be carried out. This comprehensive study will have two aims. First, Chapter 7 highlighted that one of the barriers to equitable distribution might be a perception of lack of capacity, rather than an actual lack of capacity. A comprehensive study will help to dispel any uncertainty regarding countries' capacity to participate in the CDM. Second, the comprehensive study should identify which countries lack CDM capacity and in what areas they require capacity support (such as capacity to undergo the project registration process or technical capacity to develop and implement projects). This will enable targeted capacity-building support to be given to these countries. Without such a study, capacity-building efforts may simply amount to 'shots in the dark', as they will be taken without a real knowledge of the areas or issues where such efforts are required.

Chapter 9 outlines that some capacity-building initiatives have been undertaken within the CDM regime and highlights the difficulty of measuring the effectiveness of these initiatives. Nevertheless, to the extent that lack of capacity and local expertise remains a barrier to CDM participation by some countries, especially those with the lowest human development, more targeted assistance is needed to help these countries improve their participation in the CDM. So far, under the CDM regime, a lot of capacity building has been provided to a wide variety of countries. Attention should now turn specifically to the countries with the greatest need.

These countries should receive concrete support to help them participate more effectively in the CDM:

(a) Such support should include raising the awareness in local project developers of the kinds of activity that would qualify as CDM projects or PoAs and working with them to identify a database of potential projects.

(b) These local project developers should then receive training in the process of preparing CDM project documentation and related activities, such as selecting baseline methodologies and establishing baselines.

(c) Lastly, in order to ensure that these lessons actually yield projects, it is absolutely crucial to work with local developers on pilot projects all through the project cycle, from beginning to end. Not only would this build the capacity of these developers, but these projects would also serve as 'pioneer' projects, hopefully catalysing even more projects in these countries.

As noted in Chapter 9, most of the capacity building so far has been provided to all developing countries, generally. However, Chapter 5 concludes that certain countries, specifically those with the greatest need, require preferential treatment to enable their effective participation in the CDM and achievement of their CDM potential. What is required is capacity building that is targeted specifically at these countries (identified in Chapter 6) and that is designed to respond to specific capacity needs (such as those identified through a comprehensive study of countries' capacity).

Undoubtedly, some developing countries, other than those developing countries with the greatest need, do lack sufficient capacity to effectively participate in the CDM. This book is not advocating depriving these countries of the opportunity to receive the required capacity building. However, because the countries with the greatest need are the ones least able to help themselves and most in need of external support, what is being advocated is targeting them for capacity-building support. Therefore, in addition to any general capacity building provided to all developing countries, targeted support should be given to those countries with the greatest need, designed specifically to address their identified capacity needs.

In conclusion, it is important to note that, when providing targeted capacity building to countries with the greatest need, the GHG emission reduction potential of these countries should also be taken into consideration. For example, there are several countries that have very low emission reduction potential. Although such countries should still receive some capacity building to help them fulfil this potential, care must be taken to ensure that they do not continue to receive capacity building to help them host CDM projects, even when they no longer have the potential to host projects. That is why countries' need *and* emission reduction potential must both be taken into consideration in efforts to address the problem of inequitable distribution.

10.2 Restricting eligibility for the CDM loan scheme

Building on the decision to provide loans to all countries with fewer than ten projects to pay for their project transaction costs, such loans should be limited to countries with the greatest need (identified in Chapter 6). This is because these are the countries that most need the financial assistance, and limiting the countries eligible for the loans will then increase the amount available to these countries. However, as highlighted in Chapter 9, such loans are only intended to cover the project transaction costs, but this is not one of the key barriers to equitable distribution. The key barrier in terms of financing is lack of finance for the project implementation costs.

10.3 Establishing a project development and implementation fund

To address the key barrier of lack of implementation costs, a mechanism similar to the loans scheme could be established, but should help finance the project implementation costs, rather than just project transaction costs. Such a mechanism should be limited to those countries with the greatest need.

This recommendation to provide access to underlying finance could be implemented in the form of a proposal made by the CDM Executive Board to COP/MOP 5, which was eventually not adopted in its original form by the COP/MOP. The proposal was for the creation of a CDM project development fund using part of the administrative proceeds of the CDM, as well as voluntary contributions from donors (EB 2009: Annex III, paragraph 7(c)). This fund was only to cover project transaction costs and capacity building, and the decision regarding providing loans to countries was probably born out of this proposal. The fund should be created, but, rather than just providing finance for project transaction costs, should provide loans sufficient to cover the project implementation costs.

It is recognised that, given the large amount of finance required for projects, this solution may not go a very long way in addressing this problem, unless enough voluntary donations are made to the fund or the loan scheme. That is why contributions to this project development fund should be made mandatory, on the basis that the aim of equitable distribution justifies requiring mandatory contributions to the fund by some parties, particularly developed country parties. We recognise that countries are usually reluctant to accede to requests for mandatory contributions, and, within the climate change regime generally, the usual practice is to 'encourage' or 'invite' contributions, usually on a voluntary basis (Decision 10/CP.7; Decision 7/CP.7; Decision 3/CP.11). Nevertheless, if countries are actually serious about promoting equitable distribution, then this is an important measure that needs to be taken to achieve this objective.

The recommendation here is, therefore, for a project development and implementation fund financed by mandatory assessed contributions from developed countries and voluntary contributions from other interested countries or entities. Eligibility to participate in the fund will be restricted to the group of countries with the greatest need, and the loans should be large enough to cover their project implementation costs. To be clear, the fund should provide loans, rather than grants, to the relevant countries, and these loans should be on favourable terms (which can be determined when designing the fund). Therefore, as the finance provided under the fund will be repaid to the donor countries, this will be close to a win–win situation, as countries will be ensuring that CDM projects are more equitably distributed among countries, and donor countries will get their money back, with some interest.

10.4 Establishing a CDM matchmaking service

A third recommendation to address the finance barrier is for the establishment of a 'matchmaking' service, similar to the CDM Bazaar, but targeted specifically at matching potential investors with projects in the countries with the greatest need. The objective of such a service would be to ensure that available CDM investment funds (as opposed to monies for purchasing CERs) are directed at, or give preference to, projects in the countries with the greatest need.

This service would maintain an up-to-date list of developed country entities seeking to invest directly in CDM projects (rather than merely seeking to purchase CERs) and link such entities to host country developers (in the countries with the greatest need) seeking financing for their projects. For example, the CDM Bazaar currently contains a list of projects, from different countries, seeking CER purchasers or investors (some of the projects are unilateral projects that have already been registered and are merely seeking purchasers for CERs generated). The Bazaar also contains a list of CER buyers wishing to buy CERs. The Bazaar, however, does not go beyond this – it is merely an information-sharing tool, making CDM information readily available to interested stakeholders.

A matchmaking service will go beyond this. It should seek both to actively source investment funds from developed country entities and also to actively match such potential investors with host country entities with CDM project ideas. For example, one of the project ideas listed on the CDM Bazaar is for an 80-MW combined cycle gas turbine in Maria Gleta, Republic of Benin (CDM Bazaar, 26 April 2013), a country classified as having very high need. It also has no registered projects and none in the CDM pipeline (CDM Pipeline, 1 March 2013). This project is listed as seeking buyers and project finance sources. A CDM matchmaking service would match the project developer with an investor seeking to invest directly in projects. Multilateral funds or investors with large portfolios (such as Vitol, Ecosecurities and EDF Trading, which are the top three buyers) would be best placed to participate in such a service, owing to the large number of projects they are involved in. They can allocate a specific percentage of their CDM funds to be used to invest directly in projects (through the matchmaking service), rather than simply to purchase CERs. However, participation should not be restricted to such funds or investors, and all investors should be encouraged to go through the matchmaking service, in order to ensure that more countries are able to participate in the CDM, particularly those with the greatest need, in order to promote a more equitable distribution of projects.

10.5 Mandating consideration of countries' sustainable development potential

We are not recommending that the CDM should no longer operate as a market mechanism. Rather, the recommendation is that the CDM should not operate like a typical market, with the only considerations being risk, cost and profit. It should operate as a mechanism that was created to fulfil environmental objectives, not market objectives. Due consideration should therefore be given to its environmental objectives of reducing GHG emissions and contributing to sustainable development, and to achieving these objectives equitably among developing countries. Consequently, this book recommends that, even as investors consider market factors such as risk and cost, they should also consider both of the CDM's objectives of reducing GHG emissions and of achieving sustainable development equitably among developing countries.

This book has defined equitable distribution of projects as a distribution that fully accounts for countries' emission reduction and sustainable development potentials. The first factor is not a problem: countries' emission reduction potential is already considered by investors. In fact, as Chapter 8 points out, it is often the only consideration, because there is no market incentive for considering countries' sustainable development potential. However, the need to achieve the sustainable development objective of the CDM, together with the fact that this objective cannot be met solely through reliance on normal market forces, justifies intervention in the market. Consequently, investors should be required to take countries' sustainable development potential into consideration when selecting countries in which to invest.

This should go beyond considering the sustainable development potential of projects, as this could just lead to more sustainable projects in the same countries already dominating the market.[1] Instead, in keeping with the factors to be considered for achieving an equitable distribution of projects discussed in Chapters 5 and 6, countries' need should be considered, and preference should be given to those countries with the greatest need. When investing in countries, investors should consider why that particular country is the most appropriate, given its human development level and need.

---

1   There is nothing wrong with this. The issue is that those countries that are underperforming should also have the chance to fulfil their CDM potential.

Currently, before a CDM project can be registered, the host country DNA must confirm that the project will contribute to its sustainable development (Decision 3/CMP.1, Annex, paragraph 40(a)). In addition, information is also provided in the PDDs, outlining how the project contributes to the host country's sustainable development and how it will result in reduced GHG emissions. Similarly, investors can be required to provide information on the reason for their choice of host country (considering the country's level of development) and explain how they have taken the country's sustainable development potential into consideration. This information should be reported in the PDDs.

This can be done on the basis of one of the proposals considered by countries for the post-2012 CDM regime, which was not adopted at the time the new regime was established. This proposal, which parties discussed during COP/MOP 6 in November 2010 and in subsequent meetings, is that developed countries should take reasonable measures to increase the number of project activities, either in LDCs, SIDS, African countries and countries with fewer than ten registered projects; or in those developing countries defined in Convention Article 4.8 (Document FCCC/KP/AWG/2010/CRP.4/Rev.4, Chapter III, paragraph 12).

In selecting and implementing such measures, the focus should be on countries with the greatest need, rather than all LDCs, SIDS, African countries, countries with fewer than ten registered projects or countries defined in Convention Article 4.8, as is the current proposal. This is because, as explained in Chapter 5, these groups include countries such as Singapore, Barbados and Qatar, which, although they are SIDS (Barbados and Singapore) or have fewer than ten projects (Qatar), have low need because of their high development index. Focusing specifically on countries with the greatest need will ensure that developed countries will be considering the sustainable development objective of the CDM, rather than just normal market factors.

A very good example of this is Phase III of the EU ETS. For new projects registered from 1 January 2013 to be automatically eligible to participate in the scheme, such new projects must be hosted in LDCs. The only CERs from new projects registered after 1 January 2013 that will be eligible for automatic inclusion in the scheme will be CERs generated from projects in LDCs (Directive 2009/29/EC: 68 and 77).

Considering that the EU ETS is the biggest market for CERs, this measure should, hopefully, spur the registration of projects in LDCs. To be effective, this kind of measure would need to be applied in conjunction with the provision of financial support to LDCs to register and implement projects (such as through a project development fund, as recommended above). Otherwise, as one of their greatest challenges is the lack of finance for the project implementation costs, this measure might still not have the desired effect.

Multilateral funds (such as the various carbon funds of the World Bank) or investors with large portfolios (such as Vitol) are probably in the best position to invest in a spread of countries, because of the large number of projects they are involved in. These should be required to ensure their projects are spread equitably across many countries, rather than keeping to just a few countries.

If investors are required to consider, not only countries' GHG emission reduction potentials, but also their sustainable development potentials, the question is how this would benefit investors. The benefit of considering the emission reduction potential is fairly obvious. A country with greater emission reduction potential will have more potential to generate large amounts of CERs, and investors can, for example, take advantage of greater economies of scale. If this is combined with better capacity and institutions, then the investor will benefit from less risk and more profit. Taking account of a country's need will not produce any of these benefits. How, then, can this be made attractive for investors, particularly those that are in the CDM market to make profit (as many of the market participants appear to be)? Considering that there is no real benefit to investors of taking sustainable development potential into consideration, especially when this may necessitate investing in countries that can only produce less profitable projects, there is a risk that a requirement of this sort may drive investors away from the CDM market. However, as discussed above, using the CDM saved developed country entities an estimated US$3.6 billion in the first commitment period, 2008–12. Although this requirement might lead to lower cost savings or profits, this would not be an unreasonable outcome, as the ultimate goal is to ensure that the objectives of the CDM are being equitably achieved. There would still be everything to play for: profits to be made, and compliance cost savings to be achieved. Therefore, this requirement should be imposed on the CDM market, despite concerns that it might reduce investors' interest in the market.

10.6 Promoting the CDM as socially responsible investing

The reason why the requirement to take sustainable development potential into consideration might drive some investors away is because of the particular focus of this market, which is to make the most profit at the least cost (as is the case with many markets). However, having a market that has a different focus may result in a different outcome. Or, to put it more accurately, the CDM market needs the right focus. It needs to focus, not on maximisation of profit (and minimisation of risk and cost), but on ensuring achievement of its environmental objectives of reducing GHG emissions and promoting sustainable development, which should be done equitably among developing countries. Although making a profit and reducing risk and cost could be part of the focus of the market, it should not be, as it is now, the primary focus. One way of addressing this issue is by promoting the practice of socially responsible investing (SRI) within the CDM.

Socially responsible investments can be said to refer to investments that combine social, environmental or ethical criteria with financial objectives (Waring and Edwards 2008: 135). In addition to their desire to minimise cost and make a profit, socially responsible investors also desire to make improvements, through their investments, to, among other things, the environment and social issues. Specifically, they aim to ensure that their investments do not conflict with their social, moral, ethical or other values (O'Brien Hylton 1992–1993: 7; Rapaport and Peebles 1992: 58). For these investors, making a return on their investments, though an important aim, is not the overriding concern.

The situation with CDM investors should be similar – the overriding concern of CDM investors should not be making a profit, but achieving the objectives of the CDM, which are to achieve GHG emission reductions and promote sustainable development, rather than to generate profit for investors. According to Sjöström and Welford, SRI 'entails that investors complement financial analysis with environmental and social criteria in order to evaluate companies for possible inclusion in an investment portfolio' (Sjöström and Welford 2009: 278). Likewise, when including CDM projects in their CDM portfolio, CDM investors should use, not only financial criteria (of minimising cost and maximising profit), but also the environmental criteria of reducing GHG emissions and promoting sustainable development equitably among developing countries.

An example of SRI within the CDM could be said to be that facilitated by the CDM Gold Standard Foundation. The Gold Standard Foundation operates the Gold Standard certification scheme, which was established to ensure that CDM projects not only produce cost-effective emission reductions, but also foster sustainable development in the host developing countries, thereby producing high-quality projects. To achieve this, project developers are required to use Gold Standard methods and tools, including a bottom-up, integrated approach that puts particular emphasis on incorporating feedback from local stakeholder consultations, and the Sustainable Development Matrix. Although the Gold Standard has a good objective and contributes to ensuring that the CDM achieves its sustainable development objective, its objectives do not necessarily including ensuring an equitable distribution of projects (although it does aim at ensuring 'equality of access for all market participants'). What is required within the CDM regime is more than this – there is a need for efforts to ensure, not only that the CDM achieves its sustainable development objective, but also that this is done equitably among all developing countries, including those with the greatest need, which have, to date, been mostly left out of the CDM market. The Gold Standard model can be improved upon to achieve this objective.

Research shows that SRI does not necessarily have a negative impact on investors' financial returns. Although not necessarily giving investors a better return for their money, SRI does not automatically result in underperforming investments (Rapaport and Peebles 1992: 59; Schueth 2003: 193). Other research has shown that SRI can only be as financially profitable as traditional investing in an inefficient market (O'Brien Hylton 1992–1993: 35). Whatever the case may be, the fact remains that, for the CDM, the only consideration cannot be financial, as that is not the sole purpose of the CDM. In fact, some could say the purpose of the CDM *does not* include profit-making, but that, in terms of cost, it only aims to help developed countries to reduce GHG emissions more cost-effectively than they can achieve domestically. Because investing in some of the countries currently underperforming could involve taking on greater risk and higher costs, it is possible that the overall financial profitability of projects in such countries may be lower than in the countries currently doing very well. But, as noted above, for socially responsible investors, the financial returns are not the overriding concern, and should not be in the case of the CDM, which has other, non-financial, objectives.

If the concept of SRI is introduced into the CDM market, with an emphasis on effectively considering the sustainable development objective of the CDM and ensuring that more countries are able to participate in the CDM, this could reduce the focus of the market on financial incentives and refocus the market more effectively on the CDM's environmental objectives of promoting sustainable development (and GHG emission reductions) equitably among developing countries. Whereas there is possibly no legal solution to effectively ensure consideration of this, practical solutions include investors or groups taking the initiative to build on the CDM Gold Standard model, but specifically with the aim of ensuring that those countries that are underrepresented in the CDM, particularly those with the greatest need, are helped to increase their level of CDM participation. This recommendation would complement, not replace, the mandated consideration of countries' sustainable development, as promoting the CDM as SRI, on its own, may not be sufficient to redirect investors' attention towards those countries with the greatest need.

10.7 Limiting the percentage of unilateral projects

The most obvious solution to the problem of the prevalence of unilateral projects in the CDM market, which is one of the key barriers to the equitable distribution of projects, is requiring that a specific percentage of all registered projects must be bilateral in the real sense (as described in Chapter 8) and, where the projects are multilateral, they should be funded by the multilateral investor, rather than by the host country entity itself. Essentially, this means requiring that, in a specific percentage of registered projects, the developed country counterpart must invest directly in the underlying project, rather than simply purchasing CERs generated from the projects.

There are different ways this can be achieved:

(a) One way is requiring that x per cent of registered projects must be bilaterally funded. This can be done, for example, by taking the average number of projects registered monthly or annually and requiring that at least x per cent of this number be bilaterally funded.

(b) A second way is requiring that x per cent of CERs used by developed countries to fulfil their emission reduction objectives are obtained from bilaterally funded projects. This option is similar to, yet fundamentally different from, a proposal previously considered by countries. This proposal was to 'require' or 'encourage' developed countries to 'take reasonable measures' to ensure that at least 10 per cent of CERs used to comply with their reduction commitments are generated from projects in either LDCs and African countries, or in countries with fewer than ten registered project activities.[2] However, this proposal would not effectively address the equitable distribution problem, because, in implementing this proposal, the CERs used could be CERs generated from unilaterally developed and funded projects – this proposal does not imply that these CERs must be from bilaterally funded projects. What is, therefore, required is a way of ensuring that more bilaterally developed and funded projects enter into the CDM market than currently obtains.

(c) This proposal provides a third way of ensuring more bilateral projects – requiring that x per cent of CERs used by developed countries are from projects developed and financed by these countries themselves (rather than by host country entities) in the countries with the greatest need (identified in Chapter 6). This option will indirectly ensure that there are more bilaterally developed and funded projects in the CDM market and will, in any event, directly improve the CDM participation of these countries and ensure a more equitable distribution of projects, which is the ultimate objective.

These three options (requiring that x per cent of registered projects be bilaterally funded; requiring that x per cent of CERs used by developed

---

2   See 'Documentation to facilitate negotiations among parties: Emissions trading and the project based mechanisms' (FCCC/KP/AWG/2010/6/Add.3, 29 April 2010), paragraph 12. Many countries objected to this option. According to some, establishing a quota is not appropriate for a market-based mechanism. During the discussions of this issue at COP 15 in December 2009 (at which the author was present), Grenada expressed reservations as to the appropriateness of establishing quotas within a market-based system. One country preferred the option of 'encouraging' countries to take reasonable measures, and several countries opposed prescribing a specific percentage of CERs to be generated from countries with fewer than ten registered projects. See, generally, Akanle *et al.* (2009).

countries to fulfil their emission reduction objectives be obtained from bilaterally funded projects; and requiring that x per cent of CERs used by developed countries be generated from bilaterally funded projects hosted in the countries with the greatest need) will greatly help to address the problem of inequitable distribution of projects, specifically by overcoming the barrier of the dominance of unilateral CDM projects in the CDM market.

The question is whether these options, or any of them, would be acceptable to countries. The first two options are probably the ones that can be designed in a way that would be most effective and most acceptable to countries. This is because, first, these options are not directly prescriptive and do not directly contradict the market nature of the CDM. They do not directly provide that there must be a limit to the number of unilateral projects or unilateral CERs, or that developed countries must invest in certain developing countries (or refrain from investing in certain countries). Instead, these options would require a certain minimum number of bilateral projects or amount of bilaterally generated CERs in the CDM market. Particularly considering that the CDM was originally intended as a mechanism under which projects would be bilaterally developed and funded, these options do not appear to be extreme or contrary to the intention or ethos of the mechanism. They would merely be to the effect that the CDM should operate more in the way it was originally intended to operate.

These options, however, may not directly improve the participation of those countries with the greatest need, as developed countries, in complying with the options, may simply increase their investments in the countries already performing well under the CDM. There is a real chance of this happening, and that is why these options should be used in conjunction with that proposed above – requiring investors to consider countries' sustainable development potential and need, to encourage them to increase their investments in those countries with the greatest need.

The last option, that of requiring investment in certain countries, may be less appealing to investors, because of its more prescriptive nature. This option is a stronger version of that proposed in section 10.5 above (relating to the market-based nature of the CDM), which is to the effect that developed countries should consider developing countries' sustainable development potential when selecting countries in which to invest. An outright prescriptive proposal may be less acceptable. Nevertheless, this is a compelling recommendation, because its implementation would go a long way in ensuring a more equitable distribution of projects than the current distribution.

11 Conclusion

The focus of this study has been on identifying how to ensure that the CDM is achieving an equitable distribution of CDM projects. It identifies two key factors that must be taken into consideration if the regime is to achieve distributive justice: countries' emission reduction potential and their need. Effective consideration of these two factors would mean that projects are more equitably spread among countries. It concludes that, to do this, certain regulations need to be introduced into the market. It also acknowledges that some of these regulations, such as requiring investors to consider countries' sustainable development potential and limiting the percentage of unilateral projects permitted under the CDM, are regulations that would ordinarily not be made in a typical market. The book points out, however, that the CDM is not a typical market, but a mechanism established to achieve environmental objectives, using a market system, and that this justifies these non-typical regulations.

To reach these conclusions, this book started by explaining the reason why countries are striving for an equitable distribution. It noted, in Chapter 2, that the CDM provides many benefits to developing countries, such as increased employment, access to energy and investment, and these are benefits that most countries justifiably want to enjoy. Ensuring an equitable distribution of projects would ensure that all countries, not just a select few, have the opportunity to enjoy these benefits. It pointed out, however, that 'equitable distribution' is undefined under the CDM regime, making the goal, together with the necessary efforts to achieve the goal, unclear.

Following on from this, Part II of this book focused on ascertaining the meaning of equitable distribution. It found that, in international law, distributive justice does not have a specific outcome (such as equal distribution), but takes a 'process-based' approach, in which a set of factors relevant to the particular issue are taken into consideration. There is, therefore, no 'one-size-fits-all' outcome that would apply to all issues and in all situations. Applying this approach to the CDM, this book identified that the two factors that should be considered are countries' emission reduction potential and need (sustainable development potential), which should be supported by giving preferential treatment to those countries with the greatest need. Using these factors, it was able to determine conclusively that the current distribution of projects is inequitable because it is not consistent with these factors.

Knowing the factors that should be considered to achieve equitable distribution and knowing that the current distribution is, in fact, inequitable made identifying the barriers to equitable distribution possible. Part III identified lack of technical capacity, the size of projects and lack of finance for project transaction and implementation costs as some of the barriers to equitable distribution of projects, all of which affect and undermine both the emission reduction potential and need factors for achieving equitable distribution. These barriers showed that the fundamental reasons why the CDM is not achieving an equitable distribution are the dominance of unilateral projects in the CDM market and the market nature of the CDM. These two elements have resulted in the countries with the lowest sustainable development potential being unable to effectively participate in the CDM. Unfortunately, the CDM regime is doing nothing to address these barriers, and, without intervention, these countries will continue to be deprived of the benefits the CDM provides.

To overcome these challenges, Chapter 10 suggested certain measures that can be put in place: capacity building; restricting eligibility for the CDM Loan Scheme; establishing a project development and implementation fund; establishing a CDM matchmaking service; promoting the CDM as socially responsible investing; mandating consideration of countries' sustainable development potential; and limiting the percentage of unilateral projects. Noting that the last two recommendations, in particular, may not be considered suitable for a typical market, it pointed out that the CDM *is not* a typical market, but a mechanism established under an environmental treaty (the Kyoto Protocol) to achieve the objectives of that treaty.

Boyd *et al.* (2007: 23) state that, 'it is logical that private investors focus their efforts on countries with low political and economic risks for their projects, and the CDM is no different in this regard from other forms of foreign investments'. The fact, however, is that the CDM *is* different from other forms of foreign investment – its goals are to achieve GHG emission reductions and sustainable development, not to generate the most profit at the lowest costs and risk. These are the objectives of the CDM, and whatever measures are needed to ensure it achieves these objectives should be taken.

Enabling all countries to participate effectively in the CDM and helping those with the greatest need to increase their level of participation will contribute to achievement of both objectives of the CDM. It will not affect the GHG reduction objective, as, even if the projects are small-scale projects, the projects will still reduce GHG emissions in these countries. It will, very importantly, also help fulfil the sustainable development objective, as it will result in more countries, particularly those that need it most, being able to participate in the CDM and enjoy its sustainable development benefits.

Appendix A
List of eligible developing countries

Eligible developing countries (KP ratification and DNA establishment)

Total = 129 (25 March 2013)

1	Albania
2	Algeria
3	Angola
4	Antigua and Barbuda
5	Argentina
6	Armenia
7	Azerbaijan
8	Bahamas
9	Bahrain
10	Bangladesh
11	Barbados
12	Belize
13	Benin
14	Bhutan
15	Bolivia
16	Bosnia and Herzegovina
17	Botswana
18	Brazil
19	Burkina Faso
20	Burundi
21	Cambodia
22	Cameroon
23	Cape Verde
24	Chad
25	Chile
26	China
27	Colombia
28	Comoros

29   Democratic Republic of the Congo
30   Costa Rica
31   Côte d'Ivoire
32   Cuba
33   Democratic People's Republic of Korea
34   Djibouti
35   Dominican Republic
36   Ecuador
37   Egypt
38   El Salvador
39   Equatorial Guinea
40   Eritrea
41   Ethiopia
42   Fiji
43   Gabon
44   Gambia
45   Georgia
46   Ghana
47   Grenada
48   Guatemala
49   Guinea
50   Guinea-Bissau
51   Guyana
52   Haiti
53   Honduras
54   India
55   Indonesia
56   Iran (Islamic Republic of)
57   Iraq
58   Israel
59   Jamaica
60   Jordan
61   Kenya
62   Republic of Korea
63   Kuwait
64   Kyrgyzstan
65   Lao People's Democratic Republic
66   Lebanon
67   Lesotho
68   Liberia
69   Libya
70   The former Yugoslav Republic of Macedonia
71   Madagascar
72   Malawi
73   Malaysia

74	Maldives
75	Mali
76	Mauritania
77	Mauritius
78	Mexico
79	Mongolia
80	Montenegro
81	Morocco
82	Mozambique
83	Myanmar
84	Namibia
85	Nepal
86	Nicaragua
87	Niger
88	Nigeria
89	Oman
90	Pakistan
91	Panama
92	Papua New Guinea
93	Paraguay
94	Peru
95	Philippines
96	Qatar
97	Republic of Moldova
98	Rwanda
99	Saint Lucia
100	Samoa
101	São Tomé and Principe
102	Saudi Arabia
103	Senegal
104	Serbia
105	Sierra Leone
106	Singapore
107	Solomon Islands
108	South Africa
109	Sri Lanka
110	Sudan
111	Suriname
112	Swaziland
113	Syrian Arab Republic
114	Tajikistan
115	United Republic of Tanzania
116	Thailand
117	Timor-Leste
118	Togo

119 Trinidad and Tobago
120 Tunisia
121 Turkmenistan
122 Uganda
123 United Arab Emirates
124 Uruguay
125 Uzbekistan
126 Vietnam
127 Yemen
128 Zambia
129 Zimbabwe

Appendix B

Eligible developing countries and their GHG emissions

GHG emissions values of all CDM eligible developing countries; Serbia and Montenegro calculated jointly, not separately

	Country	GHG emissions (2005)
1	China	7,187.00
2	Brazil	2,841.90
3	Indonesia	2,041.90
4	India	1,866.10
5	Mexico	683.4
6	Republic of Korea	568.7
7	Iran	555.9
8	Nigeria	455.3
9	South Africa	422.8
10	Saudi Arabia	376.6
11	Malaysia	358.4
12	Thailand	351.1
13	Argentina	349.5
14	Congo, Dem. Republic	269.3
15	Myanmar	261.7
16	Pakistan	240
17	Egypt	222.8
18	Philippines	208.9
19	Bolivia	201.9
20	Uzbekistan	180.9
21	Vietnam*	177.8
22	Colombia*	176.8
23	Zambia**	157.5
24	United Arab Emirates*	156.9
25	Peru	145.7
26	Bangladesh*	142.2
27	Algeria*	137.2
28	Angola* **	133.3
29	Ecuador	127.3
30	Sudan* **	122.6
31	Iraq*	121.8
32	North Korea	118.4
33	Tanzania	109.9

continued . . .

Continued

	Country	GHG emissions (2005)
34	Cambodia	106.8
35	Cameroon	106.7
36	Turkmenistan	91.4
37	Guatemala	89.4
38	Kuwait*	88.2
39	Chile*	84
40	Israel*	81.7
41	Ethiopia*	73.5
42	Syria* **	70.4
43	Libya* **	67.3
44	Zimbabwe**	65.6
45	Honduras**	62.9
46	Serbia and Montenegro* **	62.9
47	Morocco* **	60.8
48	Qatar* **	58.9
49	Papua New Guinea**	52.6
50	Oman* **	48.4
51	Singapore*	48.4
52	Azerbaijan*	47
53	Uruguay*	42
54	Kenya* **	41.3
55	Cuba* **	40.8
56	Nepal*	40.4
57	Trinidad and Tobago* **	36.1
58	Tunisia* **	33.5
59	Cote d'Ivoire* **	31
60	Madagascar* **	30.7
61	Uganda*	30.6
62	Mongolia*	30.3
63	Yemen* **	29.3
64	Paraguay* **	28.2
65	Dominican Republic* **	26.8
66	Sri Lanka* **	25.1
67	Mozambique* **	24.4
68	Jordan*	22.6
69	Mali* **	22.3
70	Senegal*	21.6
71	Ghana* **	21.3
72	Bahrain* **	21.3
73	Chad* **	20.9
74	Bosnia and Herzegovina* **	19.8
75	Lebanon* **	19.6
76	Guinea* **	19.2
77	Burkina Faso* **	17.9
78	Laos*	17.3
79	Gabon* **	14
80	Nicaragua* **	13.5
81	Moldova*	12.5

continued . . .

Continued

	Country	GHG emissions (2005)
82	Jamaica* **	11.9
83	Botswana* **	11.7
84	Namibia* **	11.6
85	Macedonia, FYR*	11.2
86	Benin* **	10.9
87	El Salvador* **	10.9
88	Panama* **	10.5
89	Costa Rica* **	10.2
90	Tajikistan*	9.8
91	Kyrgyzstan*	9.7
92	Equatorial Guinea* **	9.3
93	Albania*	9.1
94	Georgia*	9
95	Mauritania* **	8.9
96	Armenia*	7.4
97	Haiti* **	7.4
98	Niger* **	7.3
99	Malawi* **	6.9
100	Togo* **	6
101	Guyana* **	5.3
102	Eritrea* **	4.2
103	Solomon Islands* **	4.2
104	Rwanda* **	3.8
105	Mauritius* **	3.8
106	Sierra Leone* **	3.6
107	Suriname* **	3.6
108	Fiji* **	2.7
109	Swaziland* **	2.7
110	Burundi* **	2.6
111	Bahamas* **	2.3
112	Guinea-Bissau* **	2
113	Liberia* **	1.9
114	Bhutan* **	1.7
115	Timor-Leste***	1.7
116	Lesotho* **	1.6
117	Barbados* **	1.5
118	Gambia* **	1.3
119	Djibouti* **	1.2
120	Belize* **	1.1
121	Maldives* **	0.7
122	Cape Verde* **	0.5
123	Antigua and Barbuda* **	0.5
124	Saint Lucia* **	0.4
125	Samoa* **	0.3
126	Grenada* **	0.3
127	Comoros* **	0.3
128	São Tomé and Principe* **	0.2

Notes: * Data from land-use change and forestry not available; ** PFC, HFC & SF6 data not available; *** CO_2 data only.

Appendix C

Eligible developing countries and their HDI

HDI values of all CDM eligible developing countries, except the Democratic People's Republic of Korea

	Country	HDI
1	Republic of Korea	0.909
2	Israel	0.900
3	Singapore	0.895
4	Qatar	0.834
5	Barbados	0.825
6	Chile	0.819
7	United Arab Emirates	0.818
8	Argentina	0.811
9	Bahrain	0.796
10	Bahamas	0.794
11	Uruguay	0.792
12	Montenegro	0.791
13	Kuwait	0.790
14	Saudi Arabia	0.782
15	Cuba	0.780
16	Panama	0.780
17	Mexico	0.775
18	Costa Rica	0.773
19	Grenada	0.770
20	Libya	0.769
21	Malaysia	0.769
22	Serbia	0.769
23	Antigua and Barbuda	0.760
24	Trinidad and Tobago	0.760
25	Albania	0.749
26	Georgia	0.745
27	Lebanon	0.745
28	Iran	0.742
29	Peru	0.741
30	Macedonia	0.740
31	Mauritius	0.737
32	Bosnia and Herzegovina	0.735
33	Azerbaijan	0.734
34	Oman	0.731

continued . . .

Continued

	Country	HDI
35	Brazil	0.730
36	Jamaica	0.730
37	Armenia	0.729
38	Saint Lucia	0.725
39	Ecuador	0.724
40	Colombia	0.719
41	Sri Lanka	0.715
42	Algeria	0.713
43	Tunisia	0.712
44	Belize	0.702
45	Dominican Republic	0.702
46	Fiji	0.702
47	Samoa	0.702
48	Jordan	0.702
49	China	0.699
50	Turkmenistan	0.698
51	Thailand	0.690
52	Maldives	0.688
53	Suriname	0.684
54	Gabon	0.683
55	El Salvador	0.680
56	Bolivia	0.675
57	Mongolia	0.675
58	Paraguay	0.669
59	Egypt	0.662
60	Moldova	0.660
61	The Philippines	0.654
62	Uzbekistan	0.654
63	Syria	0.648
64	Guyana	0.636
65	Botswana	0.634
66	Honduras	0.632
67	Indonesia	0.629
68	South Africa	0.629
69	Kyrgyzstan	0.622
70	Tajikistan	0.622
71	Vietnam	0.617
72	Namibia	0.608
73	Nicaragua	0.599
74	Morocco	0.591
75	Iraq	0.590
76	Cape Verde	0.586
77	Guatemala	0.581
78	Timor-Leste	0.576
79	Ghana	0.558
80	Equatorial Guinea	0.554
81	India	0.554
82	Cambodia	0.543
83	Lao	0.543

continued ...

Continued

	Country	HDI
84	Bhutan	0.538
85	Swaziland	0.536
86	Solomon Islands	0.530
87	São Tomé and Principe	0.525
88	Kenya	0.519
89	Bangladesh	0.515
90	Pakistan	0.515
91	Angola	0.508
92	Myanmar	0.498
93	Cameroon	0.495
94	Madagascar	0.483
95	Tanzania	0.476
96	Nigeria	0.471
97	Senegal	0.470
98	Mauritania	0.467
99	Papua New Guinea	0.466
100	Nepal	0.463
101	Lesotho	0.461
102	Togo	0.459
103	Yemen	0.458
104	Haiti	0.456
105	Uganda	0.456
106	Zambia	0.448
107	Djibouti	0.445
108	Gambia	0.439
109	Benin	0.436
110	Rwanda	0.434
111	Côte D'Ivoire	0.432
112	Comoros	0.429
113	Malawi	0.418
114	Sudan	0.414
115	Zimbabwe	0.397
116	Ethiopia	0.396
117	Liberia	0.388
118	Guinea-Bissau	0.364
119	Sierra Leone	0.359
120	Burundi	0.355
121	Guinea	0.355
122	Eritrea	0.351
123	Mali	0.344
124	Burkina Faso	0.343
125	Chad	0.340
126	Mozambique	0.327
127	Congo DR	0.304
128	Niger	0.304

Bibliography

Ahnish, F.A. (1994) *The International Law of Maritime Boundaries and the Practice of States in the Mediterranean Sea*, Oxford: Oxford University Press.

Akanle, T., Appleton, A., Kulovesi, K., Schulz, A., Sommerville, M., Spence, C. and Yamineva, Y. (2009) *Summary of the Copenhagen Climate Change Conference.* Online. Available at: www.iisd.ca/download/pdf/enb12459e.pdf (accessed 2 May 2013).

Akanle, T., Kulovesi, K. and Mead, L. (2008) *Summary of the Africa Carbon Forum.* Online. Available at: www.iisd.ca/africa/pdf/arc1501e.pdf (accessed 3 March 2013).

Amr, M.S. (2002) 'Diversion of international watercourses under international law', *African Yearbook of International Law*, 10: 109–79.

van Asselt, H. (2009) *The EU ETS in the European climate policy mix: past, present and future.* Online. Available at: http://papers.ssrn.com/sol3/papers.cfm?abstract_id=1596892 (accessed 29 March 2013).

Baumert, K.A., Kete, N. and Figueres, C. (2000) *Designing the clean development mechanism to meet the needs of a broad range of interests.* Online. Available at: http://pdf.wri.org/cdm_design_note.pdf (accessed 30 April 2013).

Birnie, P., Boyle, A.E. and Redgwell, C. (2009) *International Law and the Environment*, 3rd edn, Oxford: Oxford University Press.

Boyd, E., Hultman, N.E., Roberts, T., Corbera, E., Ebeling, J., Liverman, D.M., Brown, K., Tippmann, R., Cole, J., Mann, P., Kaiser, M., Robbins, M., Bumpus, A., Shaw, A., Ferreira, E., Bozmoski, A., Villiers, C. and Avis, J. (2007) *The clean development mechanism: an assessment of current practice and future approaches for policy.* Online. Available at: www.tyndall.ac.uk/sites/default/files/wp114.pdf (accessed 20 March 2013).

Boyle, A. and Freestone, D. (eds) (1999) *International Law and Sustainable Development: Past Achievements and Future Challenges*, Oxford: Oxford University Press.

Busse, M. and Hefeker, C. (2007) 'Political risk, institutions and foreign direct investment', *European Journal of Political Economy*, 23: 397–415.

Capoor, K. and Ambrosi, C. (2008) *State and Trends of the Carbon Market 2008*, Washington: World Bank.

Cazorla, M. and Toman, M. (2000) 'International equity and climate change policy', *Climate Issue Brief*, 27: 1–20.

Christopherson, M. (1996) 'Toward a rational harvest: The United Nations Agreement on Straddling Fish Stocks and Highly Migratory Species', *Minnesota Journal of Global Trade*, 5: 357–80.

Churchill, R.R. and Lowe, A.V. (1999) *The Law of the Sea*, 3rd edn, Manchester: Manchester University Press.

Cosbey, A., Parry, J., Browne, J., Babu, Y.D., Bhandari, P., Drexhage, J. and Murphy, D. (2005) *Realizing the development dividend: making the CDM work for developing countries*. Online. Available at: www.iisd.org/pdf/2005/climate_realizing_dividend_sum.pdf (accessed 25 June 2013).

Cosbey, A., Ellis, J., Malik, M. and Mann, H. (2008) *Clean energy investment: project synthesis report*. Online. Available at: www.iisd.org/pdf/2008/cei_synthesis.pdf (accessed 23 March 2013).

Cullet, P. (1999) 'Equity and flexibility mechanisms in the climate change regime: conceptual and practical issues', *RECIEL*, 8: 168–79.

Cullet, P. (2003) *Differential Treatment in International Environmental Law*, Aldershot: Ashgate Publishing Limited.

Curnow, P. and Hodes, G. (eds) (2009) *Implementing CDM Projects: Guidebook to Host Country Legal Issues*, Roskilde: UNEP.

Dias, R.A., Mattos, C.R. and Balestieri, J.A.P. (2006) 'The limits of human development and the use of energy and natural resources', *Energy Policy*, 24: 1026–31.

Dundua, N. (2006–2007) *Delimitation of maritime boundaries between adjacent states*. Online. Available at: www.un.org/Depts/los/nippon/unnff_programme_home/fellows_pages/fellows_papers/dundua_0607_georgia.pdf (accessed 30 April 2013).

Dupasquier, C. and Osakwe, P.N. (2006) 'Foreign direct investment in Africa: Performance, challenges, and responsibilities', *Journal of Asian Economics*, 17: 241–60.

Egede, E. (2011) *Africa and the Deep Seabed Regime: Politics and International Law of the Common Heritage of Mankind*, Dordrecht: Springer.

Ellis, J., Winkler, H., Corfee-Morlot, J. and Gagnon-Lebrun, F. (2007) 'CDM: taking stock and looking forward', *Energy Policy*, 35: 15–28.

Ellis, J. and Kamel, S. (2007) *Overcoming barriers to clean development mechanism projects*. Online. Available at: www.oecd.org/dataoecd/51/14/38684304.pdf (accessed 20 March 2013).

Errin, S. (1984) 'Law in a vacuum: the common heritage doctrine in outer space law', *Boston College International and Comparative Law Review*, 7: 403–32.

Frakes, J. (2003) 'The common heritage of mankind principle and the deep seabed, outer space, and Antarctica: will developed and developing nations reach a compromise?', *Wisconsin International Law Journal*, 21: 409–34.

Freestone D., Barnes, R. and Ong, D. (eds) (2006) *The Law of the Sea: Progress and Prospects*, Oxford: Oxford University Press.

French, D. (2000) 'Developing states and international environmental law: the importance of differentiated responsibilities', *International and Comparative Law Quarterly*, 49: 35–60.

French, D. (2005) *International Law and Policy of Sustainable Development*, Manchester: Manchester University Press.

Gillenwater, M. and Seres, S. (2011) *The Clean Development Mechanism: a review of the first International Offset Program*. Online. Available at: www.c2es.org/docUploads/clean-development-mechanism-review-of-first-international-offset-program.pdf (accessed 5 May 2013).

Globerman, S. and Shapiro, D. (2002) 'Global foreign direct investment flows: the role of governance infrastructure', *World Development*, 30: 1899–919.

Grzybowski, A., McCaffrey, S.C. and Paisley, R.K. (2010) 'Beyond international water law: successfully negotiating mutual gains agreements for international watercourses', *Pacific McGeorge Global Business & Development Law Journal*, 22: 139–54.

Guruswamy, L.D. (1999–2000) 'Climate change: the next dimension', *Journal of Land Use & Environmental Law*, 15: 341–82.

Gwage, P. (2012) *Suppressed demand: unlocking climate finance for Africa.* Online. Available at: http://cdkn.org/2012/04/suppressed-demand-in-climate-change-negotiations/ (accessed 3 May 2013).

Habib, M. and Zurawicki, L. (2002) 'Corruption and foreign direct investment', *Journal of International Business Studies*, 33: 291–307.

Hailun, Y.G. (2012) 'Measuring and monitoring energy access: Decision-support tools for policymakers in Africa', *Energy Policy*, 47: 56–63.

Halvorssen, A.M. (2005) 'The Kyoto Protocol and developing countries – the clean development mechanism', *Colorado Journal of International Environmental Law and Policy*, 16: 353–76.

Halvorssen, A.M. (2007) 'Common but differentiated commitments in the future climate change regime – amending the Kyoto Protocol to include Annex C and the Annex C Mitigation Fund', *Colorado Journal of International Environmental Law and Policy*, 18: 247–66.

Holden, P. (2004) *Government reforms to reduce transaction costs and promote private sector development.* Online. Available at: www.cipe.org/publications/papers/pdf/IP0406.pdf (accessed 22 March 2013).

Huq, S. (2002) *Applying sustainable development criteria to CDM projects: PCF experience.* Online. Available at: www.iied.org/pubs/pdfs/G00083.pdf (accessed 8 May 2013).

IEA (2012) *World Energy Outlook 2012*, Paris: OECD Publishing.

ILA (2002) 'New Delhi Declaration of Principles of International Law Relating to Sustainable Development', *International Environmental Agreements: Politics, Law and Economics*, 2: 211.

Jahn, M., Michaelowa, A., Raubenheimer, S. and Liptow, H. (2003) *Climate protection programme: unilateral CDM – chances and pitfalls.* Online. Available at: www.giz.de/Themen/en/dokumente/en-climate-unilateral-cdm.pdf (accessed 23 March 2013).

Joyner, C.C. (1998) *Governing the Frozen Commons: The Antarctic Regime and Environmental Protection*, South Carolina: University of South Carolina Press.

Kossoy, A. and Guigon, P. (2012) *State and Trends of the Carbon Market 2012*, Washington DC: World Bank.

Kwiatkowska, B. (2001) 'Equitable maritime boundary delimitation – a legal perspective' in H. Caminos (ed), *Law of the Sea*, Aldershot: Ashgate Publishing.

Lecocq, F. and Ambrosi, P. (2007) 'The clean development mechanism: history, status, and prospects', *Review of Environmental Economics and Policy*, 1: 134–51.

Loibl, G. (2004) 'The evolving regime on climate change and sustainable development' in N. Schrijver and F. Weiss (eds), *International Law and Sustainable Development: Principles and Practice*, Leiden, Boston: Martinus Nijhoff Publishers.

Lutzeyer, S. (2008) *Climate trading: the clean development mechanism and Africa.* Online. Available at: http://ideas.repec.org/p/sza/wpaper/wpapers60.html (accessed 30 April 2013).

McCaffrey, S.C. (2003) *The Law of International Watercourses: Non-Navigational Uses,* Oxford: Oxford University Press.

McCarthy, J.J., Canziani, O.F., Leary, N.A., Dokken, D.J. and White, K.S. (eds) (2001) *Climate Change 2001: Impacts, Adaptation, and Vulnerability: Contribution of Working Group II to the Third Assessment Report of the Intergovernmental Panel on Climate Change,* Cambridge: Cambridge University Press.

McGillivray, M. (1993) 'Measuring development? The UNDP's Human Development Index', *Journal of International Development,* 5: 183–92.

Maggio, G.F. (1996–7) 'Inter/intra-generational equity: current applications under international law for promoting the sustainable development of natural resources', *Buffalo Environmental Law Journal,* 4: 161–224.

Metz, B., Davidson, O.R., Bosch, P.R., Dave, R. and Meyer, L.A. (eds) (2007), *Climate Change 2007: Mitigation, Contribution of Working Group III to the Fourth Assessment Report of the Intergovernmental Panel on Climate Change,* Cambridge: Cambridge University Press.

Michaelowa, A. (2005) *CDM: current status and possibilities for reform.* Online. Available at: www.hwwi.org/uploads/tx_wilpubdb/HWWI_Research_Paper_3.pdf (accessed 8 May 2013).

Michaelowa, A. (2007) 'Unilateral CDM – can developing countries finance generation of greenhouse gas emission credits on their own?', *International Environmental Agreements,* 7: 17–34.

Muller, A. (2007) 'How to make the clean development mechanism sustainable – the potential of rent extraction', *Energy Policy,* 35: 3203–12.

Newell, P. (2012) 'Of markets and madness: whose clean development will prevail at Rio+20?', *Journal of Environment & Development,* 21: 40–3.

O'Brien Hylton, M. (1992–1993) '"Socially responsible" investing: doing good versus doing well in an inefficient market', *American University Law Review,* 42: 1–52.

OECD/IEA (2007) *World Energy Outlook 2007,* Paris: International Energy Agency.

Oppenoorth, H., Koene, M. and Staarink, I. (2007) *The Bali guide on CDM: towards a sustainable CDM.* Online. Available at: http://archief.snm.nl/pdf/klimaattopbali_brochure_bali_guide_def_webversie_copy.pdf (accessed 8 May 2013).

Oude Elferink, A.G. (1994) *The Law of Maritime Boundary Delimitation: A Case Study of the Russian Federation,* Dordrecht, Boston, London: Martinus Nijhoff Publishers.

Paulsson, E. (2009) 'A review of the CDM literature: from fine-tuning to critical scrutiny?', *International Environmental Agreements,* 9: 63–80.

Pfeifer, G. and Stiles, G. (2008) *Carbon finance in Africa – a policy paper for the Africa Partnership Forum.* Online. Available at: www.africapartnershipforum. org/meetingdocuments/41646964.pdf (accessed 25 June 2013).

Pitelis, C. (ed) (1993) *Transaction Costs, Markets and Hierarchies,* Oxford and Cambridge: Blackwell Publishers.

Pittock, A.B. (2005) *Climate Change: Turning up the Heat,* London: Earthscan.

Prouty, A.E. (2009) 'The clean development mechanism and its implications for climate justice', *Columbia Journal of Environmental Law,* 34: 513–40.

Rajamani, L. (2006) *Differential Treatment in International Environmental Law*, Oxford: Oxford University Press.

Rapaport, M.S. and Peebles, J. (1992) 'Socially responsible investment', *Probate and Property*, 6: 58–61.

Sagara, A.D. and Najam, A. (1998) 'The human development index: a critical review', *Ecological Economics*, 25: 249–64.

Sands, P. (2003) *Principles of International Environmental Law*, 2nd edn, Cambridge: Cambridge University Press.

Schachter, O. (1991) *International Law in Theory and Practice*, Dordrecht: Martinus Nijhoff Publishers.

Schueth, S. (2003) 'Socially responsible investing in the United States', *Journal of Business Ethics*, 43: 189–94.

Segger, M.C. and Khalfan, A. (2004) *Sustainable Development Law: Principles, Practices & Prospects*, Oxford: Oxford University Press.

Sengupta, A. (2002) 'On the theory and practice of the right to development', *Human Rights Quarterly*, 24: 837–89.

Shelton, D. (2007) 'Equity' in D. Bodansky, Brunnée, J., and Hey, E. (eds), *The Oxford Handbook of International Environmental Law*, Oxford: Oxford University Press.

Sieghart, L.C. (2009) 'Unilateral clean development mechanism – an approach for a least developed country? The case of Yemen', *Environmental Science and Policy*, 12: 198–203.

Sjöström, E. and Welford, R. (2009) 'Facilitators and impediments for socially responsible investment: a study of Hong Kong', *Corporate Social Responsibility and Environmental Management*, 16: 278–88.

Sutter, C. (2001) *Small-scale CDM projects: opportunities and obstacles – can small-scale projects attract funding from private CDM investors?* Online. Available at: www.up.ethz.ch/publications/documents/Sutter_2001_Small-Scale_CDM_Vol1.pdf (accessed 21 March 2013).

Sutter, C. and Parreño, J.C. (2007) 'Does the current clean development mechanism (CDM) deliver its sustainable development claim? An analysis of officially registered CDM projects', *Climatic Change*, 84: 75–90.

UN (2006) *Secretary-General's Address to the UN Climate Change Conference*. Online. Available at: www.un.org/apps/sg/sgstats.asp?nid=2303 (accessed 11 November 2012).

UNDP (2003) *The Clean Development: A User's Guide*, New York: UNDP.

UNDP (2010) *Human Development Report 2010, The Real Wealth of Nations: Pathways to Human Development*, New York: UNDP.

UNDP (2013) *Human Development Report 2013: The Rise of the South: Human Progress in a Diverse World*, New York: UNDP.

UNEP (2009) *Primer on CDM Programme of Activities*, Roskilde: UNEP.

UNEP and Ecosecurities (2007) *Guidebook to Financing CDM Projects*, Roskilde: UNEP.

UNFCCC (2005–06) Annual Report of the Executive Board to the COP/MOP, Addendum (FCCC/KP/CMP/2006/4/Add.1 (Part I), 7 November 2006) (EB 2006). Online. Available at http://unfccc.int/resource/docs/2006/cmp2/eng/04a01p01.pdf (accessed 1 August 2013).

UNFCCC (2009) Annual Report of the Executive Board to the COP/MOP (FCCC/KP/CMP/2009/16, 4 November 2009) (EB 2009). Online. Available at http://unfccc.int/resource/docs/2009/cmp5/eng/16.pdf (accessed 1 August 2013).

UNFCCC (2012) *Benefits of the Clean Development Mechanism 2012*. Online. Available at: http://cdm.unfccc.int/about/dev_ben/ABC_2012.pdf (accessed 3 March 2013).

UN General Assembly, 22nd Session, First Committee, Official Records, Doc. A/C.1/PV.1515, Official Records. Online. Available at www.un.org/depts/los/convention_agreements/texts/pardo_ga1967.pdf (accessed 1 August 2013).

University of Cambridge (1992) *International Boundary Cases: The Continental Shelf*, vol. 1, Cambridge: Grotius Publications Limited.

Waring, P. and Edwards, T. (2008) 'Socially responsible investment: explaining its uneven development and human resource management consequences', *Corporate Governance: An International Review*, 16: 135–45.

Table of international treaties and other instruments

Table of cases

Table of UNFCCC documents and decisions

Index

For Product Safety Concerns and Information please contact our EU
representative GPSR@taylorandfrancis.com
Taylor & Francis Verlag GmbH, Kaufingerstraße 24, 80331 München, Germany

www.ingramcontent.com/pod-product-compliance
Lightning Source LLC
Chambersburg PA
CBHW070805290326
41931CB00011BA/2144

* 9 7 8 1 1 3 8 9 3 7 4 9 9 *